GW00357171

HOMAGE

JOHN QUINN
HOMAGE
A Salute to Fifty Memorable Minds

VERITAS

Published 2023 by
Veritas Publications
7–8 Lower Abbey Street
Dublin 1, Ireland

publications@veritas.ie
www.veritas.ie

ISBN 978 1 80097 074 8

10 9 8 7 6 5 4 3 2 1

Cover images: *Beacon of Hope* by Andy Scott, Belfast, Sergi Reboredo/Alamy Stock Photo/HDTA30; 1937 3d stamp celebrating Bunreacht na hÉireann/Richard J. King, Department of Posts and Telegraphs/Wikimedia.

Lines from *A Tribe Apart: A Journey into the Heart of American Adolescence* by Patricia Hersh (p. 21), Ballantine Books, 1999.

Lines from *The Will to Live* by Seán Boylan and John Quinn (pp. 58–65), The O'Brien Press, 2006. Used with permission.

Lines from *The Works in Verse and Prose Complete of the Right Honourable Fulke Greville, Lord Brooke* (p. 94), 1870.

Lines from *All Souls* and 'The Letter' by Michael Coady (pp. 109–10 and pp. 111–14) from *All Souls* (1980) and *Oven Lane* (1987). Used by kind permission of the author and The Gallery Press, Loughcrew, Oldcastle, County Meath, Ireland, www.gallerypress.com.

Lines from *The Irish Language in a Changing Society: Shaping the Future*, ed. Antoine Ó Coileáin (pp. 123–4), Bord na Gaeilge, Dublin, Ireland, 1986.

Lines from 'The Rock' by T.S. Eliot (p. 140) from *The Complete Poems and Plays of T.S. Eliot*, Faber & Faber, 2004. Used with permission.

Lines from *Finnegans Wake* by James Joyce (p. 143), Faber & Faber, 1939.

Lines from 'Living Ghosts' by Brendan Kennelly (pp. 240–1) from *Familiar Strangers: New & Selected Poems 1960–2004*, Bloodaxe Books, 2004. Used with permission. www.bloodaxebooks.com.

Lines from 'Memory of Brother Michael' by Patrick Kavanagh (p. 266) are reprinted from *Collected Poems*, edited by Antoinette Quinn (Allen Lane, 2004), by kind permission of the Trustees of the Estate of the late Katherine B. Kavanagh through the Jonathan Williams Literary Agency.

Lines from *Vive Moi! An Autobiography* by Seán Ó Faoláin (pp. 335–42), Hart-Davis, 1964.

Every effort has been made to contact the copyright holders of material reproduced. If any infringement of copyright has occurred, the owners of such copyright are requested to contact the publishers.

A catalogue record for this book is available from the British Library.

Designed and typeset by Padraig McCormack
Printed in Ireland by Watermans Printers Ltd, Cork

Veritas Publications is a member of Publishing Ireland.

Veritas books are printed on paper made from the wood pulp of managed forests. For every tree felled, at least one tree is planted, thereby renewing natural resources.

CONTENTS

RTÉ RADIO SOURCES

A Cork Childhood

A Portrait of the Artist as a Young Girl

All Souls

Children Reading

Heroes and Heroines

Millennium Minds

My Books, My Friends

My Education

My Millennium

Profiles from the Past

The Great Educators

The Open Mind

The Tinakilly Senate

This Place Speaks to Me

Three Men Standing at the Met

To Cure and To Care

Travels with Ben

Wonderland or Wasteland?

INTRODUCTION

In the course of a twenty-seven-year career in radio broadcasting, it was my privilege to meet and interview many interesting people. They came from very varied fields – the arts, education, politics, business, science, economics. Some spoke reflectively on their experiences and influences in their chosen careers. Others shared their visionary views for the future. In this book I am pleased to pay homage to a selected fifty contributors with excerpts from interviews, talks and writings they made available to me. In each case there is a background note on the contributor and his/her offering. In two cases – the Céifin Institute and the Class of '61 – I pay homage to a group rather than an individual. In all cases I thank the contributors for their generosity in time and interest.

I hope the assembled contributions make an anthology of ideas and experiences that will be of interest and appeal to a wide readership. For me it was a privilege and a pleasure to harvest these contributions and I am honoured to share them in print.

JOHN ABBOTT

Although born in England, John Abbott is a graduate
of Trinity College Dublin. He pursued a long career
in education as a teacher and headmaster before
becoming director of Education 2000, which
involved nine community-wide education projects
in the United Kingdom. Later, as president of the
21st Century Learning Initiative, he lectured and
wrote about new understandings of learning. His
books include *The Child is Father of the Man: How
Children Learn and Why* and (with Terry Ryan)
*The Unfinished Revolution: Learning, Human
Behavior, Community, and Political Paradox*. He
gave the 2001 Open Mind Guest Lecture entitled
'Overschooled but Undereducated? – The Struggle
for Balance in Education'. The following excerpts
are from that lecture.

Overschooled but Undereducated?

This is not meant to be an attack on schools, nor will it in any way seek to diminish the role of teachers. You must understand that I, as a one-time teacher, believe, as did the ancient Greeks, that the education of the young is so important that only the wisest members of a society should be entrusted with their nurture. Nevertheless, my belief in the importance of my profession has never prompted me to minimalise the importance of parents. We teachers tend to see individual children for only a few of the dozen or so years they spend in school. Furthermore, we see them, in the main, in the context of a classroom.

I need to share two thoughts with you. It has only been in the past 150 or so years that 'school' has figured largely in human experience. While it's true that the human brain is the most complex organism in the universe, and that brains are all to do with learning, please remember that, for 99.9 per cent of human history, our brains have been shaped by learning on the job, not by out-of-context instruction. Schools, even now, are not the only place where people learn, and many cognitive scientists see as many limitations in classroom-based instruction as they see opportunities.

Abraham Lincoln was an outstanding president of his country, yet he had only a year's schooling. In the

1620s a million or so visits were made to the London theatre by people willing to stand for three or four hours to watch a Shakespeare drama but, and it's a staggering thought, less than half of them could read or write. But they were intelligent and shrewd observers of the human condition. Never assume that learning and schooling are necessarily synonymous.

Now: a simple statistic. However you do the calculation, there is no child in an OECD country who, between the ages of five and eighteen, spends more than 20 per cent of its waking hours in a classroom. Once you have allowed for weekends, holidays and time before and after school each day, you can't get that figure any higher. Fully three-quarters of a child's waking hours are not under the direction of a teacher. To a greater or lesser extent, if they are under the direction of anyone at all, they are under the direction of parents.

As both a teacher and a father I have often made awful, embarrassing mistakes. Yet it is parents who are there before a child first encounters a teacher; it is they who are around in the evening, at the weekends and during the holidays. It is we parents who need to be there at 3 o'clock in the morning when an anguished teenager comes face to face with a reality they can't stick. Or we should be.

You had better be clear about what I mean by 'education'. I take the Latin word *educare* not only as the root of the word 'education', but also as defining its fullest meaning. *Educare* meant 'to lead out', in the sense of a Roman general leading his troops from the security of the camp onto the open field of battle. Knowing that his soldiers have been well trained, such a general was confident that they could apply such learning to the complex challenges of a tough life. Each soldier had been prepared both to stand on his own feet and to work as [part of] a team. He knew what was good about tradition, but also knew how new traditions were made. That's what I mean by 'education': preparing young people to become capable adults who can stand on their own feet, and can do better than their teachers.

Eric Hoffer expressed this brilliantly when he said, 'In times of change learners inherit the earth while the learned find themselves beautifully equipped to deal with a world that no longer exists.'

The easiest predisposition to understand is the young child's ability to learn language, apparently spontaneously. By the age of three or four, children have little difficulty in speaking their own language, while those who live in multi-ethnic environments can frequently speak two or three more languages by the age of five. In comparison to the difficulty I had in learning Latin at the age of sixteen, the young child's ability to learn language seems amazing. It is.

We now know some of the reasons why this is so. In the ancestral environment from which we came, life was highly precarious. To increase the chances of survival, people banded together into small groups and, in their search for new food sources, became of necessity nomadic and collaborative. We humans evolved as a 'small group' species, happiest, it seems, when we work in teams and multi-task. It is no accident that cricket and soccer teams have eleven players or that there were twelve disciples, or that a jury comprises twelve people. Indeed, when more than fifteen people make up a nation's cabinet, they frequently split into warring factions. Add dependents – women, children and the old – and our ancestors frequently had to deal with no more than sixty people in a lifetime.

Once humans learned to talk, we developed the most awesome new survival techniques. Let me explain. The person who can't talk, and can't understand what is said to them, is totally dependent on their own experiences to guide their actions. They know nothing they have not personally experienced. But the person who can talk can add enormously to their own experiences by adding the ideas told to them by others. Language enables us to develop a kind of 'group brain' – our thoughts are more than just our own experience.

Every child is born with this generic language predisposition. Just what they do with it depends on the culture into which they are born. Research four years ago carried out by the Kellogg Foundation in Michigan into what are the best predictors of success after the age of eighteen showed that it was the quality and quantity of dialogue in a child's home before the age of five that was four times more significant than any other factor, far more significant than either the primary or secondary school. In reality, our ancestors knew this long ago. St Augustine was said to have remarked, 'I learnt most, not from those who taught me, but from those who talked with me.' That monk understood the proper balance between formal teaching and spontaneous learning. This is the balance we have to regain.

As a parent and teacher, there is no age group that fascinates me as much as adolescents: that restless, ever questioning, bombastic but extremely vulnerable energy that never stands still long enough for us to define! In years gone by, every tribe or small community was ultra dependent on this bloody-minded energy for its survival. Adolescents played an essential role in those societies, doing things that older, more sober-minded adults would no longer do themselves. George Washington was appointed surveyor general of the Dominion of Virginia on his seventeenth birthday; the average age of Spitfire and Hurricane pilots in the Battle of Britain was nineteen and a half, and more than half of those killed in the American Civil War were under the age of twenty.

Nowadays we tend to speak not about adolescents, but about teenagers.

In an attempt to continuously 'professionalise' adult employment, we often argue that a young person should not go into work until he or she has both a university degree and some form of post-university experience. Full-time jobs for many don't start until twenty-two, twenty-three or twenty-four. The gap between being a child and full adulthood has lengthened to nearly fifteen years.

Teenagers are a by-product of contemporary society; a society so determined to get the most out of life now that we no longer have the time or the inclination to provide adolescents with apprenticeships that will fit them for a more distant future. We don't quite know what to do with teenagers any more; their energy so often goes to waste.

Frequently, their ostentatious confidence antagonises the older generations, and they bore themselves with self-indulgence. They don't have a role in society that is in any sense useful. They really do feel incomplete. And so do we, as we realise that we are no longer part of that interconnected world that was our ancestors' way of transmitting the wisdom of the ages.

Long before I became a headmaster, I knew from hard experience that it was the child who came to school already enthusiastic to make sense of issues that matter to them personally who takes from formal schooling whatever it can offer to help them meet their personal objectives. It's not the other way round, however hard the school might try.

The greatest incentive to learn is personal, it is intrinsic. That is why a caring, thoughtful, stimulating life – a life of manageable, child-like proportions – in the greater community is so vitally important. Vitally important, that is, both to the child and to societies such as our own that are so dependent, year after year, on the continuous, restless energy of the next generation of young minds.

That is why society has to realise that streets that are unsafe for children to play around are as much a condemnation of failed policy as are burned-out teachers or inadequate classrooms.

***

In his seminal study on adolescents, published in 1984, Mihaly Csikszentmihalyi, the chairman of the Committee on Human Development at the University of Chicago, noted that, on average, American fathers were, at that stage, spending less than five minutes a day in solo contact with their adolescent children. As Patricia Hersh states in her study *A Tribe Apart*,

> the most stunning change for adolescents today is their aloneness. The adolescents of the 90s are more isolated and more unsupervised than (their predecessors) ... not because they come from parents who don't care, from schools that don't care, or from a community that doesn't value them, but rather because there hasn't been time for adults to lead them through the process of growing up.

In a sense, we have to go back to the future to regain our balance. We have to recognise – indeed we have to shout it out from the rooftops and the church steeples – that schools can't do in 20 per cent of a child's working hours that which the community is no longer doing in the remaining 80 per cent of those hours. Csikszentmihalyi again:

> In all societies since the beginning of time adolescents have learned to become adults by observing, imitating, and interacting with adults around them. The self is shaped and honed by feedback from men and women who already know who they are, and can help the young person find out who he or she is going to be.

Ladies and gentlemen. Heed this warning. The proper education of our young people is our greatest responsibility. You cannot, nor should you even try, to delegate all of that responsibility to schools to do on their own.

JONATHAN BARDON

Jonathan Bardon (1941–2020) was born in Dublin. Upon graduation from Trinity College Dublin, he embarked on a teaching career in Belfast, becoming a much-respected historian and author. Among his acclaimed books are *A History of Ulster*, *Belfast: 1000 Years* and *A History of Ireland in 250 Episodes*. He also wrote many programmes for BBC radio and television and was awarded an OBE for services to community life. His contribution here is based on an interview with me from the year 2000 for the radio series *My Millennium*.

A Thousand Years of Ulster

I will attempt to draw the graph of Ulster's history over the past millennium. No easy task but there were various peaks and troughs that I hope to highlight.

A thousand years ago, Ulster was still under attack from the Vikings, bringing their ships up the Lagan and the Bann. They had a fleet in Lough Neagh and they attacked Armagh but, in fact, the Ulstermen were very successful at expelling them. In a way, though, Ulster lost out twice. The great monasteries of Bangor and Derry were destroyed but at the same time Ulster didn't get the benefit of Viking towns and cities as Leinster and Munster did. In the eleventh and twelfth centuries, the Norman incursions only managed to ensconce themselves along the coastlands of Antrim and Down. At the same time, a dramatic improvement in climate meant good weather and better crops in the farmlands of Ulster resulting in more prosperity. Later still in the Middle Ages, the Gaelic lords of Ulster drove out most of the Normans. The O'Neills burst out from Tyrone and moved eastwards to build up the great lordship of Clandeboye. A definite trough followed at the end of the sixteenth century with the Nine Years War. Hugh O'Neill banded together all the Gaelic lords to win major battles like the Yellow Ford. The seventeenth century was a grim period when the English conquered Ulster by employing ruthless means such as destroying crops and cattle, leading to mass starvation. For all of Ireland, the seventeenth century was a period of great violence, partly because of English instability, although there were hopeful signs during the reign of Charles II when the population of Ulster was beginning to rise and the linen industry was becoming an important part of Ulster's economy.

At the end of that century, more violence ensued with the Williamite Wars, the Siege of Derry and so on. The Protestants of Ulster look back on the Battle of the Boyne as if it were yesterday. It is seared into their memory, a celebration of their triumph over King James, the forces of the pope and of Louis XIV.

The eighteenth century was the most peaceful period in all of modern Irish history – it was a time of rapid economic advance for the whole island. It became a kind of race between population growth and productivity. New towns were growing. There was very considerable prosperity in mid-Ulster, which was the most densely populated part of Ireland outside of the towns and cities. But the great hope and excitement of the 1790s came to grief with the bloodshed of the 1798 Rebellion. In the Middle Ages, Ulster was by far the most Gaelic province in Ireland. The English and the Normans made little impression there. The largest town was Carrickfergus, with Coleraine and Downpatrick next. All the rest were mere villages. Belfast would have had a population of a mere two hundred. The great lords lived in castles and tower houses. The English government in Dublin referred to the area as 'the great Irishry'.

The tragedy of Ulster was that it was conquered at a time of bitter religious division over most of Europe. The native Irish population of Ulster was devastated by the conquest carried out by Lord Mountjoy and Sir Arthur Chichester; the natives remained faithful to their Catholic Church. The plantation of Ulster was carried out at the same time and in the same spirit as the colonisation of America. 'Undertakers' of the Ulster Plantation had to bring in inland Scots and English who were Protestants. So we have a resentful native population who have lost their lands and planters who are outnumbered and living with a siege mentality from the start. The Plantation was most successful in Antrim and Down. West of the Bann, the Plantation came nowhere near what had been planned. By the end of the seventeenth century, the populations of planters and natives were roughly equal in number, deeply resentful and suspicious of each other. It was only in the mid-eighteenth century with the discovery of the commercial possibilities of the linen industry that the planters begin to emerge on top.

Towards the end of the eighteenth century, although Belfast was only a tenth the size of Dublin, there was a great intellectual ferment there, fuelled by contacts with America – to which a quarter of a million Ulster Presbyterians had emigrated – and trade with cities like Bordeaux. There was much sympathy with the American Revolution and then the French Revolution in 1789 led the Presbyterians in particular to feel there was an opportunity to bring about a better society in Ireland. The Society of United Irishmen was founded in a Belfast pub and Wolfe Tone (funded by the Presbyterians) published his amazing pamphlet 'An Argument on Behalf of the Catholics of Ireland'. The Presbyterians also brought about a kind of Gaelic Revival of the Irish language and Irish music. You had the Belfast Harp Festival and Bunting's remarkable collection of Irish melodies. While the United Irishmen were liberal in their ideas, they were arrogant members of the middle classes who plunged the country into a vicious sectarian war in Ulster and a revolution in the rest of Ireland. Blundering policies in Dublin Castle didn't help matters either so a lot of early optimism had evaporated by the time the Act of Union was passed in 1800.

Following the Union, there is a remarkable economic peak in eastern Ulster. Belfast becomes the fastest growing urban centre in the whole of the United

Kingdom – from 19,000 in 1801 to 340,000 in 1901. Huge shipyards, linen mills, rope factories, tobacco factory, etc. – a kind of Yokohama of the Western world. But at the same time there were troughs – abject poverty in rural Ulster which was further accentuated by the ravages of the Great Famine. Although the nineteenth century was fairly peaceful in Ireland, there were more people killed in sectarian violence in Belfast than in all the rebellions elsewhere ([Robert] Emmet, 1848, the Fenians). Politics became nationalised rather than localised and, as nationalism spread, Ulster Protestants became more alarmed at the loss of their liberty – even if there was a limited form of independence as envisaged by Gladstone under Home Rule.

The industrial success of Belfast was short-lived. It came to a juddering halt in the winter of 1920 partly due to sectarian violence and the fact that conditions of trade changed after World War I. Mass unemployment followed. Housing and health problems grew. Then came Partition. The tragedy for Ulster was that although it had a lot to be said in its favour, it was not carried out as it had been elsewhere, e.g. Upper Silesia. There was no referendum. The Boundary Commission was loaded against the Irish Free State. So Northern Ireland had a large minority which kept tensions alive. Further, the setting up of a devolved administration in Belfast was, to me, a disaster. Catholics could now say they were far better treated before Partition than afterwards. The British government took its eye off the ball and all kinds of corrupt practices and discrimination were allowed. Then the introduction of the Welfare State led to a rapid expansion of jobs and of a health service, all of which magnified unfairness. The Education Act of 1947 led to the education of a Catholic middle class who would emerge in the civil rights movement. Television brought the civil rights movement in America and the Prague Spring in Europe into Ulster homes. Ancient hatreds and problems were exposed again in 1968–69. One of Ulster's darkest periods followed. About 3,500 people were killed in appalling circumstances, fear stalking the streets, economic growth arrested. Despite the Canary Wharf bombing and the Omagh atrocity, we have a level of peace and prosperity after the Good Friday Agreement of 1998 which I haven't seen for a long time.

TOM BARRINGTON

Tom Barrington (1916–2000) was born in Dublin, just after the Easter Rising. His father was a civil servant, who imbued the young Tom with an interest in government and in public service. Tom was educated at Belvedere College, Dublin, and at University College Dublin.

After a brief spell in the business world, he entered the civil service, starting in the Department of Finance and working his way through the ranks to the position of principal. Tom played an important role in founding the Higher Civil Servants Discussion Group, which instituted high-level debate on crucial topics. In all, he spent nineteen years in the civil service before becoming the first director of the newly formed Institute of Public Administration in 1960, a position he retained until 1977. He was editor of the journal *Administration* from 1953 to 1963 and is the author of several books on Irish administration. He also wrote *Discovering Kerry: Its History, Heritage and Topography*, a Dublin man's guide to that county. Tom Barrington argued passionately for many years for real democracy in the form of proper decentralisation and an end to what he called 'the disease of congestion of government'. His contribution here comes from his 1991 interview for the series *My Education*.

A Very Civil Servant

I went to Belvedere when I was twelve, in 1928, and I was there for five years. I liked Belvedere very much. I never had any interest in sport or games and I was regarded as an oddbod in that way. I would have made a fine forward for the rugby team and all sorts of pressures were put on me, but there was no way I was going to get engaged in those rough games. I was very attached to the Jesuits and when my father died they were good to me and my brother. Again, it was the mix of tenacity and smoothness that appealed to me about them. My youth wasn't a very happy one, with Father dying so unexpectedly, and we were very poor. There were some very good friends of my father that stood by us at the time, but friends drift away and I led a rather lonely and detached sort of life. So I didn't really have a happy childhood, or young adulthood either, until I eventually got myself established.

I got a job after I left school as what you would now call a management trainee, in a small candle firm. I was there for three years and it was an interesting experience. The capacity to get things done impressed me very much. An order would come in from the parish priest for candles or altar oil and it was sent out that afternoon. However, they were still making the candles in the same way candles had been made from time immemorial, with the wick hanging down and the chaps with a scoop pouring the melted beeswax mixture.

I got into a kind of literary circle at that time. I became friendly with Gabriel Fallon and Leon Ó Broin and I met Father Senan of the *Capuchin Annual*. He offered me a job and I was greatly taken at that stage by the crazy literary life. I had started an evening course in UCD [University College Dublin] and I persuaded him to let me attend lectures and make up the time. I had set my mind on the civil service and I needed an honours degree to get in. It wasn't really like a university education – dashing in on my bicycle and listening to the lectures and dashing back to work. I didn't make any friends at college and it wasn't much of a life for me at all, except for the lecturers. I came up against George O'Brien in economics and he remained a friend. I can still remember the thrill I got from listening to John Marcus O'Sullivan doing the French Revolution – 'Don't mind if I have the year or the month wrong, but I'll tell you the day will be right and the hour of the day will be right!' I loved history and I got a great kick out of that. I did politics with Canon Denis O'Keefe. I don't think I ever understood the subject at all, but they were the most entertaining lectures. He was an extremely funny person.

Gabriel Fallon was very good to me. He took an interest in me and set about educating me. He had a beautiful collectors' edition of the novels of Thomas Hardy and I read all of them. He taught me a lot about the theatre and how to look at plays and how they were produced. Father Senan then started a thing called the Capuchin Annual Club, which comprised a lot of his contributors. We would meet every Thursday in the Father Mathew Hall and have a meal there and Frank McManus, Roibéard Ó Faracháin, Tadhg Gahan and others would come along. Father Senan was great in attracting people like Frank Sheed, the publisher, a very entertaining customer, and a lot of people [came] from abroad to visit our meetings.

I got my honours degree, so I got into the civil service. We were quite a little collection – Paddy Lynch, for instance, was the man who came first in the exam. I went into the Department of Finance. The civil service is a very civilised sort of organisation – an extraordinary level of courtesy and formal kindliness, backed up by a tremendous amount of absentmindedness in terms of human relations! I was very taken by this after the rough and tumble of the business world. We were shown around and introduced to everybody and I was assigned to Maisie Kiely, who became one of my dearest friends. It was a real kind of a master and apprentice type of thing and she took a great interest in a number of us who she thought were personable young men. If she didn't like you, on the other hand, then that was the end of you. She held a sort of salon at her flat, not in any formal sense, but she liked to give us the opportunity to meet senior civil servants and she consciously went out of her way to civilise us and acculturate us into the system of civil service. I spent three years in Finance and that was a very interesting time.

The Department of Finance has a very orderly system – I only realised this afterwards, when I moved to the Custom House. They had a tremendous filing system. You had to read the relevant file thoroughly so you knew the background and then you had to write a minute of some sort summing up what you had read and your assessment of the letter that had come in from some unfortunate department looking for money. Then that minute was appended to the file and would be passed to various superior beings who would say, 'That fellow Barrington is an awful eejit' and put snide little notes in the margin, which was very good for you because then you began to learn the game. You were supposed to use your own judgement and initiative, even if it was against the line that the department took. In those days, the department line was that any spending was a bad thing so the answer should be no, but if a good case was made then it had to be given serious consideration.

In one sense, we were at the hub of things, but, in another, we were really on the top of a mountain when all the real action was going on at the bottom. That is one of the reasons I left. The other was that there were twenty or thirty administrative officers in Finance at that time, all about the same age and all madly ambitious. A vacancy occurred in the Department of Local Government and Public Health for a private secretary to Seán MacEntee. I applied and was summoned to the Custom House, where I was interviewed by a remarkable man who was secretary of the department, called James

Hurson. I became [MacEntee's] personal secretary and was with MacEntee for a couple of years and learned an enormous amount there. I spent time with the minister and saw all the important things that were going on in the department. Because I was reputed to have the ear of the minister, everybody was very nice and anxious to explain things, so I learned a great deal about the department, which was a very diverse one in those days. MacEntee was an extremely able man. Even though he had his failings – losing his temper and that sort of thing – basically, he was an extremely intelligent man, interested in the whole business of government. Some ministers are only interested in their own department, but MacEntee liked to have a finger in every pie.

I had one great success in those days. George Bernard Shaw had a little property in Carlow which he wanted to give to the town of Carlow. He wrote to Dev [de Valera] asking him to arrange this, but there was a lot of confusion about it and, eventually, it transpired that legislation was needed. So, a message came over from the minister on a Tuesday that the bill was to be prepared straight away and got through the two houses at once. We got our bill ready and it was approved by the government at their Friday meeting. The bill was introduced in the Dáil on Tuesday, went through the Senate on Wednesday and then, by special arrangement, the President signed it on the Thursday. Shaw was delighted and wrote to Clement Attlee, the Prime Minister of England, saying, 'You really ought to learn how to get legislation through.' I always call it the Shaw/Barrington bill!

I was eventually promoted to assistant principal and found that I had a certain gift for tidying things up and making things sensible and getting people to agree to a better way of doing things. Two chaps in the customs, Pat Doolin and James Waldron, went to a lot of trouble to persuade the Association of Higher Civil Servants that they ought to take a professional interest in the civil service, apart from the matter of pay. We got together and organised the Higher Civil Servants Discussion Group in the Custom House. It made quite an impact; two or three hundred people would turn up to meetings and talk about all sorts of things.

We subsequently decided to publish some papers. I took over the job as editor of the journal *Administration*. We had a marvellous Kerryman, Michael O'Connor, who was in the publishing business and was keen to have a paper that would stir up all sorts of intellectual debate in the civil service. People seemed to think that it wouldn't be possible to have a detached and intellectual publication that was not bashing politicians or revealing State secrets!

I was a principal at that stage and getting a bit bored with the job, so I was shunted over to the town planning section. I hated town planning – it was full of artistic pretensions but had no common sense or intellectual input at all. I was beginning to become a bit of a pseudo-intellectual. I got browned off and the thought of spending years in that milieu was too much for me. By then the Institute of Public Administration had been founded on a part-time basis and a full-time director was needed, so I let it be known that I was very discontented where I was and, in the summer of 1960, I went off to become a one-man institute.

In the late '50s, I came across one book that had an extraordinary effect on me. When we were getting *Administration* on its feet, I was writing a fair bit and reading around the subject. I began to realise that I had some capacity for abstract thinking and, by an extraordinary coincidence, the librarian in Bray at that time, Máirín O'Byrne, gave my wife a book to bring home to me. It was a book called *Insight* by Bernard Lonergan, a Canadian Jesuit, and it was exactly what I needed. It gave me confidence in my writing and in arguing for the future. It had a terrible effect on my style

– for a while nobody could understand what on earth I was talking about – but, thank goodness, I eventually learned to simplify it.

Another book that influenced me was a small book that Paddy Lynch recommended to me – *Beyond the Welfare State* by Gunnar Myrdal, the great Swedish economist and social scientist. It showed how, as people became better educated and more self-conscious, central government would shed a lot of the detailed things and these would be looked after by small groups instead. The argument was that central government should be concerned about the big issues and local government should deal with everything else. As you get a more educated and informed society, people should get the opportunity to look after their own affairs. That has remained a vision for me amid all the ups and downs of the intervening years since the early '60s.

I am not too happy with the state of democracy in this country. Local government seems to be doing only about one-third of what they should be doing. We are really very backward in terms of local democracy – having the smallest number of local authorities, the smallest number of councillors, the smallest number of functions being discharged by local government, the smallest amount of money spent by local government as a proportion of public money spent and so on. If you want a country to progress, you have got to mobilise the skills and talents and enthusiasms of the people as a whole, not just of a small number of people at the centre who won't even go to the trouble of learning how to organise themselves.

There is nothing so powerful as an idea whose time has come, and I am confident that, sooner or later, the time will come for these ideas, whether in my lifetime or not. I have tried to do what I can and, if people accept these ideas now, well and good, but, if they don't, it will probably happen in the future.

THOMAS BERRY

Thomas Berry (1914–2009) was born in Greensboro, North Carolina. He was the third of thirteen children and, as he wryly observed, 'a couple more joined us from an aunt's family to ensure we never got lonesome'. He became a Passionist priest and is regarded by many as the most important Catholic thinker in ecological theology in the twentieth century. He described himself as a cultural historian, and a student of religions and cultures, particularly in China and India.

In his writing and teaching he argued for a greater understanding of and sensitivity towards the natural world. We are at the end of the Cenozoic era, which covers the evolution of the earth over the last 65 million years, a time when, for Berry, the plunder and pollution of the planet is unprecedented. He suggested that we are now entering the Ecozoic era – a time for a mutually enhancing the human–earth relationship. I was introduced to Tom Berry by the Columban priest and writer on ecology, Seán McDonagh. I had hoped for a thirty-minute interview with this remarkable man. I emerged with a three-hour conversation, which became a five-part series, *Wonderland or Wasteland?* Tom Berry's contribution here is taken from that series.

The Alienation of the Natural World

I was born shortly after the First World War began so my earliest memories are of the post-war period, early 1920s, when the contemporary world was coming into being – commercial radio programmes, the popularity of the automobile, the building of roads, the movies. It was also a difficult time for many, a lot of poverty. In North Carolina, the making of whiskey in the hills proved to be a turbulent occupation with the introduction of prohibition. It was also a great time to be a child. There was so much freedom. I could wander through the woods, wade in the streams, enjoy the natural environment – which was my basic education. School gave me no specific education about my environment. It paid attention to human writings but none to the great book of the natural world. I learned to be independent, to make my own world. It was a world that a person could dream about, brood over, wander through – so in that sense it was a rich childhood. Later, when I reflect on how I came to be so sensitive to the destructive impact of the industrial world, I see that I had a certain antipathy to that world from when I was eight or nine years old. It ultimately determined the fact that I would go into a monastery when I was twenty years old, because I could not envisage a place for me in the commercial world. I have a brooding personality and there are only two places where you can brood – prison and the monastery – so I chose the monastery! I grew up in a Protestant world – Catholics represented only a half of 1 per cent in my home place. I knew nothing about different religious orders. There happened to be a Passionist monastery nearby, so I signed up for that. It has been a benign relationship. The order is more concerned with traditional spiritual guidance, but throughout all the orders, throughout the Catholic Church, there seems to be relatively little sense of what is happening to the planet. That to me is the greatest failure of Christianity in the course of Christian history. If we lose the beauty and splendour of the natural world through pollution, the extinction of species, the toxification of the soil and our food – this is the destruction of the very sources of religion. Religion is born under the beauty and magnificence and threatening qualities of the natural world, so it is a mystery to me as to why Christians contribute so little to critiquing this situation.

After ordination I was sent to the Catholic University at Washington to be trained as a historian and it is there that I developed an interest in Asian civilisations – China and India – and I began to study Chinese and later Sanskrit languages so that I might gain an insight into how other peoples found meaning in life. It's against that background that all my thinking and writing has developed. I was greatly influenced by Teilhard de Chardin who did three things for me. (1) He was the first person who understood that the universe had, from the beginning, a psychic spiritual aspect as well as a material one. He accepted the evolutionary process fully from a very early period in the twentieth century. (2) He identified the human process with the universe process. The total evolution of the universe was involved in the emergence of the human. (3) He moved the religious issue from a dominant redemption orientation to a dominant creation orientation. Another writer to influence me was Rachel Carson with her book *Silent Spring*. As a scientist, she was first to see what was happening with chemical pesticides, like DDT, which was toxifying the whole environment. In the US in the 1930s, we were making a half-million tons of industrial chemicals. Now we are making 200 million tons annually, which the planet just cannot deal with. Rachel Carson effectively began the modern ecology movement in its active phase.

I am a cultural historian. The various cultures of the world are largely determined by their religious and spiritual orientation. I instituted the doctoral programme in the history of religions at Fordham University – the only such doctoral programme in North America. Catholics don't study religion – they study theology. I ran that course in Fordham for fifteen years and, when I retired, the course simply ended. The supreme difficulty that we are up against now can be stated quite simply – the discontinuity that we have established between the human and the non-human and the giving of all basic values and rights to the human, with no inherent values or rights to the non-human except use by the human. So there is little feeling in the Western tradition for the integral community of life, where the human sees itself as integral to the larger community of existence … this is not based on my knowledge. The most knowledgeable people on the planet, like Peter Raven, are telling us these things. Raven would argue that, given the unprecedented rate of plunder and pollution of the planet, we simply don't have time on our side. Anything that is increasing at an exponential rate (doubling every so often) is in a state of disaster. Take the Philippines, for example. At the beginning of the twentieth century, it had a population of six million people. They lived in a very fertile group of islands that was 90 per cent rainforest. The population then rose to 12 million, then 24 million, then 48 million (doubling every 20–25 years). Now it's close to 70 million. This is leading to an impasse situation. The rainforest has been largely removed. The soil has been degraded. The mangrove swamps that provided nutrients for the fish have been destroyed. The water systems have been polluted. An ever-accelerating number of people are living on a depleted body of land. That in a contained way is the fate of the planet. India is in a similar state because of the damage to its soil caused by the hybrid grain programme instituted some years ago. Its population has doubled in the last few decades. Now it is estimated that it will reach 1.6 billion before the whole economy collapses. Who will feed the people of India and China?

My generation is responsible for the current state of things. We were 'autistic' – we had no sensitivity as to what was happening to the natural world. We need firstly to recognise this – that we are in a deep cultural pathology. Then we need to identify the enormous scale of what is happening to our air, our soils, our water, our oceans. Where do we go next? I suggest we could be entering the Ecozoic era, when humans would be present on the planet in a mutually enhancing way. There are a number of conditions under which we can do this.

1. We begin to understand that the universe is a communion of subjects not a collection of objects. The human community and the natural world will go into the future as a single sacred community or we will both experience disaster on the way. We must develop a reverence for the natural world and accept guidance from that world.

2. Accept that the human is a sub-system of the earth system. We have taught agricultural practices that are trying to outdo the rhythms of the natural world that took billions of years to work out.

3. Planet earth will never again function in the future in the way it has functioned in the past. We must help the earth to heal itself; for example, the extent to which the earth can deal with radioactive waste

that we have created is something else. It may take thousands of years, maybe hundreds of thousands of years. We cannot make a blade of grass but in the future there is likely not to be a blade of grass unless we accept it, protect it, and foster it.

MAEVE BINCHY

Maeve Binchy (1939–2012) was born in Dublin. After an early career as a columnist with *The Irish Times*, she became a prolific writer of novels, short stories and plays, which were extremely popular worldwide and were translated into many languages. Among her bestselling novels are *Light a Penny Candle*, *Circle of Friends*, *Tara Road*, *Silver Wedding* and *The Lilac Bus*. She was much loved as a warm, engaging and unpretentious guest on radio and television. I featured her in the radio series *A Portrait of the Artist as a Young Girl* (about Irish women writers on their childhood) but her contribution here comes from a 1985 session in which I used one of Maeve's own recommendations for success as a writer – eavesdropping on conversations. I recorded her in conversation with a group of secondary-school students from Co. Wexford in 1983.

So You Want To Be A Writer

I'm not here today to talk to you about great literature or great style. I would never pretend for a moment to try to change your writing style. In a one-day workshop, what could I achieve in teaching you a 'prose style'? Nothing. My hope for today is to try to get you to write as clearly and as simply as possible, using your own language and feelings and to write *observantly*. The more you can observe, 'photograph' things in your mind, the better. The more you can lose as much as possible everyone else's dead ideas and instead give as much of your own observations as possible the better also. As I see it, there are three main problems in your way.

1. Timidity. We are afraid of exposing our thoughts before others. Trust me – there is nobody waiting to laugh or ridicule your writing. Everyone else is too busy thinking about what they will write.
2. Laziness. I'll do it tomorrow, during my holidays, when I'm finished school … If you are enthusiastic NOW, start writing now. The brain doesn't improve with age. We read about brain cells dying off in their thousands as we age. You are all at a bright stage of your lives. Capitalise on that by using the sharpness and freshness of your observation.

3. Fear of failure. Some of you will write better than others but how will you know if you don't try? Preferably before the brain cells start falling like dandruff ... You may be too young to write a novel. You are certainly not too young to write a short story or a 'colour' piece. I am not equipped to judge poetry so I will leave that aside.

What will help you become a writer?

1. Keeping a diary is a BIG help. I don't mean the short terse form – 'Got up at eight. Had breakfast. Met X on the way to school. His team won last night, etc.' I mean a diary where you record actual thoughts. I wish I had kept one. I only know what I looked like when I was sixteen from some terrible photos of me in a green school uniform with a big round face staring back at me. That was 1956. There was a Suez crisis and a lot of wars going on but I have no idea what I felt about those things. So keep a real diary of thoughts, feelings, reactions. You may have fears of one of your siblings coming across it and being in convulsions or looking back at the diary yourself some years later and saying to yourself, 'How could I have been so appallingly

pretentious? Did I really have views like that on the meaning of life?' Such fears are a pity because those are nonsensical reasons, really. Be grown up enough to laugh at yourself and you might even get something out of yourself. I don't want you to be too self-obsessed but you do need to know what you felt and that will make you a more interesting person. I'm still very annoyed that I can't recall my teenage feelings.

2. Keeping a book of ideas will also help. I would love if each of you got a big book for Christmas where you could keep a diary at one end and a book of ideas at the other. I jot down ideas all the time – again, partly because of the crumbling brain cells … Something you see or hear may move you at the time. Jot it down and it may come back as a story or part of a story. On my way here this morning, I passed an old man leading a very young boy by the hand down the road – probably to catch the school bus. They made a very attractive picture in the morning light but I jotted it down. Later I might wonder about it. Where are the parents? Working? Dead? Has the father emigrated? Lots of possibilities. From that one image you can see a lot of things happening in your mind. But only if you jot it down!

3. Stare at people! Look closely at their faces and try to see them more three-dimensionally than two-dimensionally! Something that will show you a little bit of the human life that's behind a face.

4. Eavesdrop on conversations! I know that all of your life you have been told that this is a VERY BAD THING to do! You must respect privacy, etc. but if you want to write about people and the dialogue they use, it is a VERY GOOD IDEA. You are catching people as they really are, not as they pretend to be. Most of us put on an act some of the time. Again, you are sharpening your observation.

5. Practise lipreading! I've learned to do it by sitting in on a lip reading class and I have followed a television series on lipreading. I used to get very irritated when I couldn't follow people's conversations. I know it's another terrible thing to do but it's very useful and enlightening as a writer. For example, when the Queen met the Pope in England recently, I could lipread their conversation. She was asking him all about the popemobile. It's silly and trivial, I know, but it was very useful in writing a colour piece.

6. Read a lot! I know you have little time to read just for pleasure but it is opening your mind to the same world you are already exploring with your observant

eyes! The world of imagination. I read a lot when I was a teen – probably because we didn't have the distraction of TV or didn't have the pressures you have at school. And we didn't see much of the world. I was forever reading. I still never go anywhere without a book in my bag. I read all sorts of stuff – some of it could be rubbish, but I read very quickly. So I would like you to try and read more. You will never be bored if you have the habit of reading.

7. Get rid of other people's (usually tired) phrases. At school we weren't good at Irish so our teacher made us memorise an entire essay, every word and phrase. In our case it was 'Glendalough'. The theory was that you could 'adapt' it in an exam situation. For example, you are asked to write an essay on 'A Surprise'. So you start off with Mammy announcing one day that you were going on a surprise trip. And where did you go? Glendalough! Problem solved! What a silly way to go! It gave us no confidence at all. Why do we do the same with English? – coming home tired but happy at the end of a wonderful day …

So please – write as you speak about what you see, hear, feel. Get rid of tired old phrases, clichés, jargon. Write simply and clearly. In one word – communicate!

SEÁN BOYLAN

Seán Boylan (*b.* 1949) was one of the most successful Gaelic football managers of modern times. He managed the Meath team for twenty-three years (1982–2005), during which time Meath reached seven All-Ireland finals, winning four of them, as well as winning four National League titles and eight Leinster championships – truly remarkable achievements. As a fellow Meathman and unashamedly one of his greatest fans, I was deeply honoured when he agreed to tell me his story, which was published as *The Will to Win* (O'Brien Press, 2006). It is, in fact, two stories, because Seán has had an equally interesting life as a herbalist. In this extract from the book, he tells of his decision to step down as manager in 2005.

Stepping Down

The introduction of the qualifier system into the All-Ireland championship was not the only change that would influence the fortunes of the Meath team. At club level the Meath county board revamped the county championship. The old system had four divisions with four teams playing each other on a league basis. It meant that a club could only afford to lose maybe one match if they wanted to progress, and so the competition was quite intense. The new format had two divisions of eight teams. This meant that a club would now play seven matches and could lose two and possibly draw another one – and still qualify for the semi-finals. I fully understood the intention behind this change, to give players more matches at club level, but to me it seemed that for the first time it was almost being bred into Meath players that it was all right to be beaten.

From a county team point of view, in the old system you timed all your preparation towards the first round of the Leinster championship and had possibly one round of the club championship before that date. Now we would have three rounds of the club championship interrupting our inter-county preparation. There was a greater danger of losing players through injury. I spoke with the county executive about this but they felt the new format was the right way to go. I told them that unless we got an extraordinary run of good fortune, it could be ten years before Meath would win a Leinster title again. I naturally hoped I would be proved wrong, but I was being practical, not defeatist.

That was only the tip of the iceberg. Most young fellows go to third-level colleges now and inter-college competitions like the Sigerson Cup are quite intense. The Sigerson Cup was once the preserve of a handful of universities, but is much wider in scope now and is taken very seriously. There have been instances where students trained for their college at 6.30 a.m. and were expected to train for the county under-21 team that evening. If you were on the county senior team you now had seven National League matches in a row during February–March. Where was the time for rest or recovery or, dare one ask, the time for study in the case of students? The situation was farcical.

Every club team now has a manager and he naturally demands his players to be present for training at that level also. For inter-county players this was a crazy set-up. These are amateur players but a professional standard was being demanded of them. In fact I doubt if professional players would be asked to subject themselves to such a rigorous regime. We were inviting trouble and we got plenty of it. Players will always pick up injuries but the scale of the problem had reached a new and frightening magnitude. When we played Dublin in the 2005 championship, we had eight players on the injured list. In 2004 there were eleven players injured. In 2003 the figure was ten. This may seem like sour grapes now, but they were the hands dealt to us.

I was disillusioned with the new club championship format from its inception and for three successive years I pleaded my case to the county executive: Pat O'Neill, central council representative; Barney Allen, county board secretary; Fintan Ginnity, chairman; and Colm Gannon, treasurer. We were playing counties in the championship whose policy was not to start their club championship until the county's involvement was over – and here we were playing club under-21 championships (which started before 17 March), county under-21 championships, club senior championships, intervarsity championships and seven National League matches – all in the run-up to the inter-county championship. It was inevitable that the injuries would mount up and players would suffer burnout. It should not have been a surprise. If, for example, a club is playing Carnaross then the mantra will be: 'Hold Ollie Murphy (Carnaross's star player) and you will win!' Naturally, Ollie will come in for more attention. We will all support Ollie when he plays for Meath, but at club level it's another story … Similarly with all inter-county players. It could be an argument for a larger panel, but I don't like too big a panel. Every player on the panel should feel he has a chance of getting on the team, otherwise it is a self-defeating exercise. In my view, the county executive should have eaten humble pie and said this new format was not working. I don't think a reversal of the format would have taken from the club championship at all. I regret that the executive did not see things my way.

From 2001 onwards I stated my case each year in an interview for the position of manager. Each nominee was interviewed and then the executive put the names before club delegates for voting. I never doubted for a minute that I could do the job, given the time and conditions to nurture promising players. Otherwise I would not have wasted anyone's time, least of all my own. I found those interviews ultimately humbling. They were probably embarrassing for the executive too, but according to the by-laws of the GAA it is the duty of the county executive to select the coach/manager. In my view they abdicated their responsibility by leaving the decision to the delegates, who had not heard my views nor those of any of the candidates. The executive should have said:

'This is the man for the job', and stick with that. Instead they were putting candidates up against one another, which led to canvassing of votes – something I abhor and never practised.

I remember the day with particular clarity, 31 August 2005. It was the day of the funeral of the great Galway maestro, Sean Purcell. I travelled with my father-in-law, George Yeates, down to Tuam to pay my respects. It was a hugely emotional day for the family and the fans of this great but humble man, and as always the Galway people made us visitors so welcome. The meeting with the county board executive later that evening was obviously on my mind, and earlier in the day I was leaning towards having one more go at the managerial job. The more I thought about it, however, the more I felt I would be wasting my time going forward.

For three years I had spoken with the executive and nothing had happened regarding the club championship. I had no power to change things. About half an hour before the meeting I made up my mind. I would stand aside and let someone else have a go at the job. I rang Tina a few minutes before going into the meeting. Her reply was simple: 'Okay, if that's how you feel, that's fine.' I rang my good friend Tommy Reilly. His reply was similar. Out of courtesy I informed my co-selector Colm

Coyle and asked him to tell the other selectors, David Beggy and Declan Mullen. I walked into the meeting and told the executive that if they felt changes could not be made, there was no point in my going ahead. 'What do we do?' Brendan Dempsey asked. 'Just say I'm not standing', I said. It was as simple as that. There was no storm-out, no histrionics. It was not an ego thing, as some journalists have written. If it were, the time to walk away would have been after some major success. I just had an obsession with sport and found great satisfaction in helping young men achieve excellence in sport. Now it was over. An amazing twenty-three-year journey had ended.

Despite being offered great hospitality in Tuam, George and I had not eaten, as we were rushing back to the meeting. We went to the County Club for a meal and did not get home until after eleven o'clock. Seán Junior and Ciarán (who should have been in bed for a very early start for school next day) were there to meet me with Tina. Seán ran to me and threw his arms about me. At the tender age of thirteen he knew the significance of the moment. The word spread quickly and early next morning Des Cahill rang me from RTÉ Radio. 'I can't believe this,' he said. 'You have been in management for as long as I have been in broadcasting!' As the morning wore on there was a stream of callers to the house: my sisters, neighbours, friends, and people who had worked with me over the years. Some people brought drink; others brought cakes and flowers. It was like a wake. The 'corpse', however, was fine. I had loved what I did, but if it was felt that I could no longer do it right, so be it. No regrets. I like to think I served my county well. It was a great honour and privilege to do so and those twenty-three years have been a fantastic part of my life.

I reflected on all those who had influenced me: my parents, teachers like Father O'Sullivan and Father Murray in Belvedere College, the great West Indian cricketer Frank Worrell (who was one of my first coaches in Belvedere), Jim McCabe and Sean Murphy in Clogher Road school, my childhood hurling hero Dessie Ferguson (whose sons I would later coach), great Dunboyne men like Brian Smith and Paddy McIntyre. I was so lucky to rub shoulders with my heroes – all of them passionate men.

Who am I after all? I am just a guy who was asked to do his best to bring success to his county. That is all I am. I was never any greater than the man who carried the bags. I was never fortunate enough to play in an All-Ireland Final, but I was lucky enough to have a team in seven All-Ireland Finals and four National League

Finals. I was blessed with the support of selectors, back-up team and the county board. I am thankful to my maker for the talents I was given. As a child I may have dreamed of lifting up the Sam Maguire Cup as Meath captain, but that is not the hand I was dealt. We all have our different talents. I just thank God for those that were given to me and that I had the opportunity to use them. It is hard to believe that a little leather bag of air, with 'O'Neills' written on it, could evoke such passion and endeavour, such goodwill when you were successful and the opposite when you made a mess of it … But isn't it wonderful that it is so?

Looking back on my career with Meath, it was quite simply a labour of love. Love of sport. Love of making it happen for willing young players. Love of place and of what success did for your people – and being sorry as hell when it didn't happen for them! No matter which way it went, love was at the heart of it all.

JEROME BRUNER

In the mid-1980s I was in West Cork to record an interview with Mary Norton, author of the classic children's novel *The Borrowers*. I was invited to stay for lunch, during the course of which Mary's husband said to me, 'You're involved in education. Do you know that just a few miles from here there lives one of the great educationists of our time – Jerome Bruner?' I did well not to choke on my apple crumble, but he was right. Jerome Bruner had a summer house in Glandore. I made contact with him and interviewed him a number of times. On one occasion he suggested I initiate a debate on the school curriculum for the twenty-first century. There were, in fact, five such debates in the radio programme *Education Forum* and Jerome Bruner gave an overview in 1982 on the issues emerging from the debates. That overview is the basis for his contribution here.

Jerome Bruner (1915–2016) was born in New York. He was educated at Duke and Harvard universities and his research work on psychology and education made him one of the most respected figures in those fields. He spent eight years at Oxford University when his focus was on early language development. On his return to the United States, he joined New York University's School of Law. He lived for over a century, dying in 2016. Thankfully for me, he spent many summers in Glandore, where I was privileged to avail of his wisdom.

A View from The Outside

I enjoyed the five programmes thoroughly. At a transition time like this, one hopes for consciousness-raising, getting the matters in hand discussed in an open-minded fashion, and that's what I sensed in these programmes. There were five main issues that emerged.

1. Continuity. The need for continuity between what is taught at primary and secondary levels is important. Equally, the continuity of relationship between school and work. We need to question also the implicit continuity that exists between the

curriculum that is put together and the expectations that somehow everybody is university-bound, whereas we know that only 11 per cent of students got to university. So there is a need to question if that curriculum is the ideal track for all students.

2. Homogeneity. Is it right that the same curriculum be followed by all students? There was a lot of discussion on the question of more local initiative, whether there should be more attention given to the gifted, the handicapped, those with specialised interests and whether those issues should also be recognised in the examination system. Christina Murphy from *The Irish Times* was particularly strong on this point.

3. The dominance of the written examination. Ireland is not alone here. There is evidence of a heavy influence from the academic world. Might we be a little more flexible with something based on practical work and in-class performance?

4. Bringing the schools more closely in touch with technology. On the one hand there was talk of making technology a subject of instruction while on the other hand there were suggestions which leaned toward media studies. An interesting problem but by no means a simple one.

5. The hidden curriculum. This related to personal development. I think it was Ivor Browne who suggested that schools should represent something closer to a caring society.

***

I would raise one preliminary question in response to these issues. Education, like all great enterprises of a culture, represents to me a predicament rather than a problem which has a unique solution. The best you can do with a predicament is to manage it and keep managing it.

A number of points emerging from these discussions intrigued me. One was how society wanted a method of certifying people, to have numbers on them which would indicate whether they would suit this job or that, while at the same time there was an effort by society to take the whole child into account. This tension always exists and I don't think one needs to despair about the fact that there is no particular solution to that problem.

I have, as many of the participants in your discussions pointed out, the sense that your education system is much too tied to a written examination, to be taken by thousands of students, in spite of the fact that you know very well that some of them will become university professors while others will be perfectly able people who are going to be farmers, electronic repairmen, etc. – all of the elements that make a society run. This is another predicament! Obviously, in order to keep a society operating effectively, you need a common focus but you also need differentiation. I feel strongly that you need diversification. I once jokingly made the comment that maybe we should have a Monday–Wednesday–Friday curriculum devoted to the liberal arts and a Tuesday–Thursday curriculum devoted to new problems that face society today. There's a range of things that we use but because we don't understand them we feel helpless. For example, a great many people don't know how a petrol engine runs, or what happens when you click on a light switch or when you turn on the radio, or even know how a bicycle works. I have always had the feeling that one of the things that ought to be done in a society is that, when you teach physics or chemistry, you should elucidate the ordinary. I would like to see more computing, more electronics, more mechanics in the science curriculum, not just as technology but as essentially the base of the curriculum. Simply put, the rendering more ordinary of the technical devices that we use, in order to give people some status beyond that of button pushers.

Another sphere which was mentioned a lot by the secondary-school students on the discussions was that some understanding of how communities run – an approach to human behaviour – needs to be incorporated in the curriculum. I wouldn't want that to be mere gossip sessions. If we're dealing with economics, for example, we should be looking at concepts like competition, what makes market forces operate imperfectly. Equally, in the human sciences, I would like to see the introduction of notions that come from anthropology and the evolution of human societies.

There were comments from the students that the teaching of English literature tended to be boring. How has that happened? I would like to see some imagination put into the teaching of the liberal arts. Regarding literature, I see on BBC television, for example, the production of modern interpretations of the plays of Shakespeare by people like Jonathan Miller. These can be very exciting – even with plays that you don't see very often, such as *Coriolanus* and *Timon of Athens*. If the school could take such plays or plays from the Abbey Theatre as a start and then get students reading as a way of conducting textual criticism, there is absolutely no reason why literature should be dull or boring. One of the reasons that literature is found to be boring is the requirement that all the representative works should be covered. Why is this considered necessary? I think if you understand half a dozen plays or novels well, you've got a key for reading for the rest of your life.

Finally, an area which came up quite a lot in these discussions – the teaching of foreign languages. I'm going to take a hard-nosed view here. We have wasted an extraordinary amount of money teaching people the bare elements of a language that might just enable them to order a meal when they go abroad. That to me is a displaced expenditure. Studies from all over the world repeatedly say not to start a language unless you are going to follow it through. Two years of language study is a waste of time. So let's say a fair proportion (10 or 15 per cent?) of students will need a foreign language to keep business or foreign services going. I would go for an intensive approach and set up a scholarship programme for interested students. There's no point at all in inserting two years of, say, German in the curriculum and hoping you're going to get a great bargain in the process. The students – apart from the rare bird who is very clever at it – will end up not knowing very much German at all and you have wasted a great amount of money – and a lot of time which could have been spent on other areas of the curriculum.

TONY BUZAN

Psychologist, writer and educational consultant Tony Buzan (1942–2019) was born in Middlesex, England. His study of the working of the human brain led him to devise ways of improving learning and memory. In particular, he popularised the technique of mind-mapping – 'a graphic technique for putting outside your head what is going on inside your head'. His eighty-plus books – some of which became million-sellers – include *Use Your Head: How to Unleash the Power of your Mind*; *The Mind Map Book: How to Use Radiant Thinking to Maximize Your Brain's Untapped Potential*; *and The Speed Reading Book: Read more, learn more, achieve more.* He lectured all over the world to government bodies, multinational companies and leading business organisations. His contribution here is based on a 1997 *Open Mind* interview about one of his books, *The Power of Spiritual Intelligence: 10 ways to tap into your spiritual genius.*

The Power of Spiritual Intelligence

Spiritual intelligence is a combination of different things. One is getting the 'big picture' – seeing yourself in relation to other things. Being compassionate towards other living things. Being charitable and being concerned. It is not necessarily being spiritual in the religious sense. It is being human on the fundamental level of living the good life. There are ten ways to tap into your spiritual intelligence.

1. Getting the big picture. Remember how, as children, we all wrote our address in full? As a seven-year-old I remember writing 'Tony Buzan, 48 Oxford St., Whitstable, Kent, England, Earth, The Universe'. My father, who made telescopes, encouraged me by letting me view the planet Saturn surrounded by its glorious rings. I realised as a young boy that there was a much bigger world out there than my home, my school, my friends. I got a sense that I was a small boy who was part of a wondrous scheme of things, but at the same time big enough to see it all. We realise that our planet is a precious jewel

and yet it is tiny in relation to the universe. We feel grand and humble at the same time. I remember interviewing Edgar Mitchell, an astronaut who travelled around the dark side of the moon. That part of the journey would take about an hour but it seemed like an age and he wondered if they were permanently trapped there. He thought of his wife, his family, his neighbourhood – all the 'big' things in his life. When they finally emerged from the dark side, there away down in his vision was this tiny blue pearl – planet Earth. He felt he could reach out and flick it away with his finger. For him it was a transforming experience – how tiny and fragile the earth was even in relation to the local universe. He became 'spiritual', devoting his life to helping other people realise the beauty and fragility of our planet. Each of us has to work on our spiritual intelligence and we must never forget what a work of art each of us is. We must value and appreciate ourselves for the amazing creatures we are.

2. Exploring our values. What do I like? What is 'good' or 'bad' to me? Am I honest with others? Just consider these things and make a mind-map of your values – a sort of graphic technique for putting outside your head what is going on inside. Then you

can decide what areas within that map you might want to focus on.

3. Have a life vision and purpose. This doesn't mean having a grand plan for saving the planet. It can be as simple as devoting yourself to the development of your family in all the ways they can possibly develop. Check your 'self-talk', the way you chat to yourself. Avoid the negatives ... be a good coach to yourself!

4. Exercise compassion. Remember John Donne's line – 'No man is an island'. See how interconnected we all are. It is a natural state to be open to other people. Learn from your mistakes and move on. Appreciate the other point of view.

5. Charity and gratitude. Giving can be easy but receiving demands a particular skill. So often, if someone pays you a compliment ('Well done. You're looking very well') we refuse to accept it. What you are actually saying – 'You're an idiot. You don't know me', etc. The other option is to say, 'Thank you so much.' It can be a difficult thing to do because we can be programmed not to think well of ourselves.

6. The power of laughter. Statistics tell us that the average child laughs three hundred times a day or more. The average university student laughs well below a hundred times a day and many business people laugh

below twenty times a day. That is horrifying because laughter is the bubbling expression of joy, happiness, energy, love. And it exercises many muscles; it is an energiser and a stress-reducer.

7. Onward to the child's playground. The child is uninhibited, spontaneous, full of enthusiasm, innocent. Why can't we try to retain that? It's a spiritual state. So often we repress those feelings as adults. Watch children on a beach – playing with grains of sand, bringing home a broken shell as a treasure.

8. The power of ritual. We need ritual in our lives. We need to strike the balance between being rigid and being totally disorganised and confused. Watch any major athlete. Each of them has different rituals they go through before they compete – blessing themselves, looking in a particular direction, etc. Birthdays, anniversaries, celebrations with friends – these are rituals which we shouldn't leave behind because they are buttresses on the architecture of our lives and they give enjoyment. Every society has rituals but the danger is that the ritual can be removed from its original purpose. It's important to reflect on the day ahead in the morning and on the day past at night.

9. Peace. Be able to be still with yourself. Prayer and meditation are examples of that. So also is being non-violent. Turn things off! Make your home a sanctuary. At least three or four times a day, create little islands in the day when you can be calm, still, reflective. Watching nature can also induce that calm we all need.

10. All you need is love. Love is a tough thing to accomplish. We need to extend every molecule of ourselves to embrace that other person, that environment. It doesn't mean being wimpish. It means being strong. It often happens in family situations that the child will constantly try to prove that the parent doesn't love it. 'You don't love me anymore', etc. All that child is really saying is, 'Please, please, please confirm that you do love me, because I'm frightened or worried.' You have, of course, to love yourself – not in the sense of being egocentric or narcissistic. It means being your own best companion, looking after yourself, appreciating the miracle you actually are, being able to accept the errors you made and learn from them. Then the two of you – you and 'your own best pal' – can go out and help others.

THE CÉIFIN CONFERENCES

Harry Bohan is a Clare-born priest who ministers in the parish of Sixmilebridge in Co. Clare. A man of considerable dynamism, energy and optimism, he devoted much of his early career to the revitalisation of rural communities, starting with his native village of Feakle. His work was always influenced by the two institutions that shaped him – family and community. These inspired him to put the heart back into rural communities by building houses and encouraging families to come back from the big industrial centres. He achieved considerable success with this venture but as the century drew to a close, and Ireland seemingly basked in the success of its Celtic Tiger economy, he took another look at our society – the changes it was undergoing, the values that shaped that change and the values that would be needed to shape our future.

So, in 1998, he founded the Céifin Centre for Values-Led Change. Céifin is the Celtic goddess of inspiration and for ten years an annual Céifin Conference was held in Ennis, Co. Clare. This was a think-tank that drew an attendance of over five hundred people and featured an extraordinary range of thinkers, critics and analysts. In 2008, I was asked to give an overview of Céifin's importance over its decade of existence. This is what I wrote.

What Céifin Means to Me

In Patrick Kavanagh's novel *Tarry Flynn*, Tarry's mother asks, 'What does it all mean?' – to which Tarry replies, 'What does anything mean? Are any of these people going anywhere except to the grave?'

For ten years now, Céifin has been engaged in the same dialogue. What does it all mean? Where are we going as a society? What is driving us? What is leading us? Does it have to be this way? I have been asked to write briefly about what Céifin means to me. I will attempt to literally spell out my answer.

C is for Connection. We live in a fast-moving, changing and competitive world. The pace of change confuses us. Our 'busyness' cuts us adrift from our fellow man and we lead isolated lives. Our competitive world sets us further apart. Community has become fractured. We are disconnected not only from each other but from the institutions – family, church, state – which hitherto held us together. Our society is akin to a splintered mirror. We need a vehicle to help us connect with ourselves and with each other, to fill the vacuum that is modern life, to piece together those splinters and hold the mirror whole to society and celebrate what is positive and good as well as highlight what is troubling and eroding. In a phrase used by Charles Handy – 'to bring our souls to light'.

Céifin *is that vehicle.*

E is for Energise. In all our modern busyness, our energy is dissipated. There are so many calls on our time and energy. We need a charger, to power our lives and energise us for directions we have forgotten or neglected. In the words of Seán Ó Riordáin, 'ní ceadmhach neamhshuim' – indifference is not allowed.

Céifin *is that charger.*

I is for Inspiration. Céifin was a Celtic goddess of inspiration. An annual inspiration or 'breathing in' of ideas, stories, reflections, comment, dialogue and debate can only be good for the national psyche. To be exposed to the contributions of people like Charles Handy, Mike Cooley, Mary McAleese, Stephen Covey, Emily O'Reilly, Joe [J.J.] Lee, Mark Patrick Hederman, Robert [D.] Putnam, Marie Murray, David McWilliams, Maureen Gaffney and many others can only enrich us individually and collectively.

Céifin *is that inspiration.*

F is for Focus. It is perhaps a sign of the times that there are few enough occasions and venues where the major issues and concerns of our society in the new millennium can be focussed upon. That focus will attract delegates from the corporate sector, the professions, administrators, and interested individuals – like the farmer who fits a national conference into the 'rhythm of the year'.

Céifin *is that focus.*

I is for Influence. Charles Handy has written and spoken extensively about 'the elephant and the flea'. The elephant is the large organisation, nowadays fragile and insecure. The flea is the individual who makes the elephant uncomfortable, and who can operate outside the organisation. Fleas influence or 'flow in' new and different thinking on individual lives, on administration and ultimately on society at large. This may happen in small ways but they are important ways. It is a ripple-in-pond situation, but ripples become waves.

Céifin *is that influence.*

N is for Narrative. Change needs to be recorded and reflected on. Each individual has a story to tell and deserves to be facilitated in telling that story. The complete 'tale of the tiger' needs to be told. Amid all the euphoria, there are things we as a society have forgotten. The published proceedings for the past ten years' conferences will be important sources and points of reference for those who will shape our society in years to come.

Céifin *is that narrative.*

ERSKINE CHILDERS

Erskine Barton Childers (1929–1996) was the third generation to bear that distinguished name. His grandfather was a politician and writer who was executed during the Civil War in 1922. His father was a Fianna Fáil politician who became the fourth president of Ireland in 1973 and died suddenly in office in 1974. Erskine Barton Childers was a writer, a BBC correspondent and a senior civil servant with the United Nations. On the recommendation of Michael D. Higgins, I invited Erskine Childers to give the 1995 Open Mind Guest Lecture, in which he spoke on 'The United Nations in the Real World'. This extract is from his 1999 contribution to the radio series *Millennium Minds*.

A Millennium Reviewed

Let us set the clock, as it were, for a review of the past thousand years. In the year [AD] 1000, the

Scandinavians were all over the place. Leif Erickson was supposedly landing in North America. The Danes, led by Sven the Forked-Beard, were conquering Norway and Sweden and had invaded the Isle of Wight. Here in Ireland, Brian of Munster [Brian Boru] was about to establish his supremacy and the Battle of Clontarf would be fought in fourteen years' time. The first potatoes were being planted, not in Ireland but in Peru, under a brilliant Tiahuanaco culture, and Mayan civilisation was at its zenith in the Yucatán Peninsula. Oxford University would not exist for another 167 years and the University of Paris not for 250 years. Ireland's monasteries were still Europe's fountainhead of academic sustenance, but there were huge and thriving Arab academies in Baghdad and beginning in Córdoba in Spain, with only one of several libraries having as many as 400,000 books, containing the assembled knowledge of accessible humankind. A gifted young Arab scientist, Ibn Sina, was beginning to write an encyclopaedia of medical knowledge that Europe would still be consulting in the 1700s. In Basra, in what we now call Iraq, the future father of the science of optics was four years old, but he would write a giant thesaurus on optics and perspective which Lorenzo Ghiberti would be annotating in Florence five hundred years later as he fashioned the relief carvings for the doors of the Baptistry. And what we now call Banking had been developed in Baghdad with the use of a piece of paper expressing committed money values which, a thousand years later, is our cheque.

All of this was immensely promising, but the beginning of the millennium also contained its warnings. In China in the year [AD] 1000, charcoal, sulphur and potassium nitrate were brought to a perfect mixture and ignited in something we would most regrettably come to call gunpowder. They didn't use the explosive brew for violence but for fireworks, but when Europe got hold of it all military hell broke loose and has never since been fully contained. So in this series about the great minds that have moved humankind during the past millennium, we have to think not in years or decades but in centuries. The millennium's astounding rate of progress, compared with previous millennia, did not happen because some significantly larger number of brilliant human beings were born during these centuries. It happened because for the first time connections were made among those minds and from them to more and more citizens of the planet until there were vastly more intellects at work, in turn making ever wider connections with others along endlessly multiplying webs of human intercourse.

The enormous changes in what we can call the human communication environment have only come recently. Consider music as a source of enlarging human sensibilities, of stretching the spiritual, artistic and creative capacities of young people to make their lives richer and, in turn, those of their children. The gramophone record, the first technology to reproduce multi-instrumental and multi-vocal music in a form accessible to families in their own homes or to students in schools, was only available in this final century of the millennium. Before then, the great performers and composers could only be heard by the very few who lived in cities where concerts of their music were performed and who could afford it. Of course, being musical was a hallmark of family life. People saved to buy a piano or violin, music lessons and the score of a great composition. But to experience a symphony requiring a full orchestra was impossible for the overwhelming majority of any population. It is a true millennial wonder that today any Irish boy or girl can listen to a variety of music, does not have to own or play a piano or violin and can know all the symphonies. If the classical giants of the music of the millennium are aware of this they will be in eternal joy, for they were forever frustrated by the limited audiences they could reach.

But what made a major mind of the millennium was almost always more than the genius and the persistence of that one individual. To begin with, they learned from and built upon the efforts of those who had come before them, but in most of the disciplines and fields of endeavour that produced these minds a complex tapestry of social, economic, political and technical factors was also essential for their work and its impact. For example, it was only because the aristocracies and the Churches were patrons of the great composers, architects and artists that we can acknowledge these immensely gifted people at the end of this millennium. For another dimension to this tapestry, the new or better sounds that they strove to create would never have reached us but for the responsive genius of craftsmen in improving musical instruments.

So then, let's reach back far down the centuries to try to weave together some of the main factors that gave individual humans the chance to make an impact on their fellow citizens and the direction of their society that we can now attribute to them. This great adventure did not begin in Europe but in the so-called Third World, when it was veritably the first world. The historian Michael Edwards has written that 'before [AD] 1500 Europe's debt to Asian sciences and technology was almost total'. First, someone had to want and then be able to reproduce sets of words as continuous text. You could not spread knowledge to many people if each book had to be hand-scribed on parchment, as in the Irish monasteries. So someone, somewhere, had to discover how to copy a text on a light, thin material that was also durable. This would be paper, which was developed in China in AD 105, using the cellulose found in hemp and cloth rags. And as our millennium opened, again in China, a man was carving individual letters on the ends of fingers of clay, baking them and sticking them side by side to make up words and then printing blocks of these on paper. We were on our way to moveable type and the information age, even if it took 400 years to get to Gutenberg's printing press in Germany.

Chinese paper and original crude printing technology were first imported into the Arab world and by [AD] 900, paper was being manufactured in Cairo. As Europe began to recover from its Dark Age, merchants needed better records and students at the new universities needed textbooks. But virtually the only available textbooks were in Arabic, so two things happened. A veritable industry of translating Arabic into Latin sprang up in Italy and Spain. Those irritatingly advanced Arabs had everything Europe needed, documented and built upon by their own scholarship. And then in Germany a new metal technology in printing was developed. In 1448 Gutenberg responded to the clamour for books, the pressure of the clergy for bibles for the faithful and the needs of business by inventing a printing press which was spread across Europe by his apprentices. Europe would never be the same again following the explosion in communication. Forty-five thousand different books were published over a period of fifty years, and there were twenty million copies of them. Newspapers followed. In America, Samuel Morse perfected an electric pulse, carried over wire, and in 1844 the telegraph arrived. In 1882, a speaker in the London House of Commons said that 'information that was once the exclusive possession of a favoured few is now the common property of all … the world has become a vast whispering gallery'. And before we knew it, we were in the age of cinema, radio and television, then [that of] the computer and satellite communications.

Shall all this sheer speed in the transmission of ideas and images end up diluting the quality of the human intellectual and artistic product? The Informatics Age is very seductive but aspects of it may also be very destructive. I think we have to mind our minds. Technology can now compress on a single silicone chip information that only thirty-five years ago needed a roomful of computers, but technology has not mutated our cortex to speed up our thought processes to keep pace with the silicon chip. In America, the soundbite is now down to eight seconds.

In 1633, Fulke Greville, a little-known English poet, wrote these words which I hope will act as a thought-provoking curtain-raiser to the series *Millennium Minds*:

> The mind of man is this world's true dimension
> And knowledge is the measure of the mind;
> And as the mind in her vast comprehension
> Contains more worlds than all the world can find
> So, knowledge doth itself far more extend
> Than all the minds of men can comprehend.

NOAM CHOMSKY

Noam Chomsky was born in 1928 and grew up in an internationally enriching Jewish tradition. At university, he became interested in the study of linguistics and developed his own radical theory, which argues that grammar is not learned from scratch but is innate. Our mental attributes, like our physiology, are determined by our genes.

He became a political activist in the 1960s and 1970s, leading the resistance to the United States' involvement in South-East Asia. He spent most of his academic career in the Massachusetts Institute of Technology. In this 1994 excerpt from the series *My Education*, he talks about the formative influence of his early education – at home and at school.

Home and School

I was born in Philadelphia, Pennsylvania. The family was essentially an immigrant family. I had one brother, five years younger, but different enough in age for us not to have grown up intellectually together. My father came from the Ukraine when he was about seventeen; my mother was actually born here, but only a year after the family had arrived from Lithuania. Both my parents were Hebrew teachers and my father was a Hebrew scholar as well as a director of the Hebrew educational system in Philadelphia. They both worked afternoons and Sunday mornings and afternoons, so we had to have household help. I actually had an Irish maid take care of me for the first couple of years of my life.

My parents sent me to a nursery school by the time I was about eighteen months old. It was a Deweyite progressive school run by Temple University as an experimental school. This was the heyday of John Dewey's educational influence and I stayed at the school from the age of eighteen months to about twelve years. I still have childhood memories of being wheeled to school in a baby carriage. Alongside that, from an early age I went to Hebrew school, where, as in the home environment, Hebrew education and the Jewish tradition were the fundamental values. It was primarily from the local Jewish community that my father's friends came, people who spoke Hebrew and were raising their children in similar circumstances.

The Dewey education was the best educational experience of my life, without any comparison. The school encouraged individual creative work, but it was completely non-competitive. When I went to the local academic high school at twelve, I realised for the first time that I was a good student. I seemed to be getting all As and other people weren't. There was a differentiation among students; people were judged by where they ranked and that was the first time that I had ever seen that happen. In the first years of my own schooling, kids had worked together and were encouraged to perform to the best of their ability and praised for what they did. It was a very healthy intellectual environment and very stimulating. I became interested in science – chemistry and natural sciences – and I remember third-grade projects on astronomy. I was quite interested in political affairs and the first article I wrote was when I was about ten years old. It was on the Fall of Barcelona, the victory of the fascists in Spain and what that meant for the future. There was one particular teacher who was quite stimulating and got me thinking about all sorts of things and at whose suggestion I skipped a year.

Going to the academic high school, which was theoretically the best high school in the city, was like entering a black hole – I remember nothing of the next four years except hating it. It was results-orientated, geared specifically to getting you through the college entrance exam with a high mark. It didn't matter if you understood anything at all or forgot about it the next week. I had to take a German exam to get into college and I had never studied German, so I literally sat and memorised a five thousand-word dictionary for the couple of weeks before the exam, got through the exam okay and then forgot it all a week later. That was considered quite acceptable, but it was quite different to the early part of my education.

I read a huge amount of nineteenth-century novels and history and science books. There was a science institute, the Benjamin Franklin Institute, in the city and by the time my friends and I were old enough to travel alone on public transport, we would spend our Saturday afternoons down there learning about this and that. It was a pretty interesting, intellectual environment. It was the end of the Depression and a very lively time in political terms – I was interested in that, at least to the extent that a pre-teenager could be.

Home was completely different. On Friday night, which is the celebration of the Jewish Sabbath, my father and I would go off together and read Hebrew novels or the Talmud. I got very immersed in late-nineteenth-century Hebrew literature – the Hebrew language was revived around the middle of the nineteenth century. Yiddish literature was being translated by authors into Hebrew and there were Hebrew poets, novelists and essayists; that was the main reading fare on those Friday evenings. By the time I was fifteen or sixteen, I was going through the literature on my own. I was very much interested in, and involved in, the Zionist movement of the day, although today it would be called anti-Zionist. It was concerned with Arab–Jewish co-operation, especially working-class co-operation. That was probably my main driving interest in my youth. I later became a youth leader and a Hebrew teacher and led such activities as discussion groups and summer camps.

None of these individual activities were exceptional, but it was unusual to have them all together. In the immigrant milieu, all the kids went to Hebrew school and studied there. I was probably doing more than others, especially studying Hebrew literature on my own. My political interests were also not unusual at that time. In retrospect, it was a funny combination of interests, but none of the individual parts were that unusual, except maybe they were more intense in my case.

THE CLASS OF '61

In 1959, I got the 'call to training' on the basis of my Leaving Certificate results. I would join 105 other young men to be trained as primary school teachers in St Patrick's College, Drumcondra. It was a two-year course, very much a 'training' programme in the old dispensation.

This was an extraordinary group of many talents. They would become diligent and inspiring teachers but they would also win acclaim as historians, writers, educators, coaches, broadcasters, actors and entertainers. Although we would only be together for two years, a terrific bond was formed among the group, a bond that would strengthen with the passing years. To mark the golden jubilee of our graduation, I compiled a celebratory volume, *Golden Threads*, to showcase their many talents. For this book, I have selected Frank Sweeney's contribution to *Golden Threads*, which gives an indication of the talents of the class of '61. Frank was a Donegal man, with an avid interest in local history. His story about his mother, Grace, illustrates how a simple event changed the lives of women in rural Donegal forever.

It's the Milkman!

Grace Sweeney is getting ready to celebrate her hundredth birthday on the 15th of December in her bungalow at Annagry in The Rosses in West Donegal. Born in 1909, she has had a varied life. She went into service or, as they called it in Donegal, went 'on hire', working for neighbours until she was sixteen. Then she worked in hotels until she departed for America in 1929, where she remained for ten years until 1939. On her return, she took over the working of the small farm of very poor land from her ageing parents. She got married in 1940 and reared four children at home, while her husband emigrated to work on the buildings in England.

When the war ended in 1945, English cities had to be rebuilt and Irish labour was required for work that lasted all year round. The tradition of seasonal migration from west Donegal to Scottish farms now gave way to year-long departures for the men, who only returned for short holidays with their wives and families at Christmas and in the summer. Consequently, the work at home was thrown on to the women, who were expected to maintain the household, rear the children and work the crops. And in this scheme of things nothing was as important as a good milking cow for family sustenance.

The cow required oats, hay, potatoes and turnips for winter feed. These had to be grown on the patches of converted bogland. Such ground was unsuitable for ploughs and all the work had to be done with the spade. But with the majority of the men over in England, many women had to do the heavy work and toil long hours in the fields.

During the '40s and '50s it was not at all unusual to see women carrying heavy creels of cow manure on their backs to the fields, or pulling harrows with ropes across their shoulders. If a man could be got for a day's work, a woman had to repay him by doing two or may three days of pulling the harrow or carrying the manure or a variety of other heavy tasks. The saving of the crops were the worst days of harvest for the women, who spent long days gathering oats, tying sheaves, building stacks and pitting potatoes and turnips. Six months of heavy labour in order that the cow could produce milk. No time for fashion, style or hairdos.

And then one day in 1961, Anthony John O'Donnell travelled around the parish with his pick-up truck filled with crates of milk. He had a team of boys with him who ran up the lanes to the houses to tell the occupants that he was selling bottles of milk and that he would come around every second day. The traditionalists were shocked. The milk could not be trusted. Nothing was as good as the milk from your own cow. It might be watered. The deliveries wouldn't last. It would ruin the place. Sure people couldn't get rid of the cows. And there were a hundred other reasons to reject the offer. It was the talk in every house at the nightly gatherings.

Grace Sweeney placed her order and collected her three bottles of milk every second day at the end of the laneway. The milk was good, better even than the milk from her own cow. And it was delivered every second day, like the man said. Spring was coming, when the delving, the harrowing, the planting and the carrying of manure would all start again. What if she got rid of the cow? The work in the field would be limited to a garden of potatoes for the household. Night after night she lay in bed pondering. She dared not let her thoughts escape to a neighbour. Her aged mother, who had laboured in the traditional manner throughout her life, would have been horrified. For weeks her dilemma tormented her.

The Dungloe fair was coming soon, on the 4th of March, so she had to make a decision. At five o'clock on the morning of the fair she was on her way to Dungloe with the cow. The price she got was not very good but the cow departed anyway. Her mother only found out on her return. There was shock. A tradition spanning the centuries had been broken. She was the talk of the place for weeks. Then her neighbour, Biddy Duffy, sold her cow and depended wholly on Anthony John's milk. With time, the talk stopped and, slowly, one by one, the women started selling the cows. Then some of the older men did likewise. Soon it became fashionable.

When discussing various aspects of her life with her family recently, Grace told us that it was not the coming of electricity to west Donegal that effected the greatest change in the lives of the people, but the coming of Anthony O'Donnell's milk lorry that dropped off the bottles of milk at the end of the laneways.

'You would know the women in the chapel on Sunday that had got rid of the cows,' she said. 'Their faces were not as haggard or as weather-beaten from being out in the fields. They didn't have as many wrinkles. That was when married women and older women took interest in their appearance. The milk changed our lives.'

MICHAEL COADY

Born in 1939, Michael has lived all his life in his beloved Carrick-on-Suir, Co. Tipperary, including a full career as a primary teacher. He is an eminent poet and writer whose many publications include *Oven Lane*, *All Souls*, *Full Tide*, *One Another* and *Going by Water*. I was privileged to collaborate with him on three memorable radio programmes – *All Souls*, *This Place Speaks to Me* and *Three Men Standing at the Met*. The latter I consider to be the nearest I have come to achieving perfection in my career as a radio producer. The following excerpt is abridged from Michael's Open Mind Guest Lecture in 2000.

Of Poetry and Place
Unlike most writers, I still live where I was born, in Carrick-on-Suir, Co. Tipperary. I have remained onsite and that compels and enables an intimate focus –

the vertical and the horizontal dimensions of place. The horizontal is what you see – the people walking around, the state of the tide on the river, who is being born or buried today. The vertical dimension is the absent presence – what lies underneath and invisibly all around; the deep, deep accumulation of lives and living on the site; what has gone before for a thousand years in terms of lives and destinies and seasons and days and nights in the exact same places with its streets and lanes straddling the same river with its cosmic dimension of its twice-daily cycle of tides and its fifteenth-century bridge over it and the fabled icon of Slievenamon behind my back as I face down river.

Coming to know a little of this river valley and town, its human timescape of memory and forgetting, is to come face to face continually with a universal and commonplace mystery – what has become of the hundreds of thousands who have lived here over the centuries? Can they still exist, in some sense? And we ourselves, the current tenants of their vacated space – why are we here? Poetry is a conduit of wonderment about the explanation of life and its meaning, an intuitive urge to utterance, a kind of singing, perhaps even a kind of prayer. It is both made and given. 'A poem is not a thing we see,' said Robert Penn Warren, 'but a light by which we may see.'

There is a unique manuscript census of Carrick-on-Suir, made in 1799, when the town had 11,000 inhabitants, twice the current population. Penned in it are the names, ages, occupations and trades of every household, every man, woman and child, including those who were blind, crippled, lunatics, paupers. Not a single hair remains of a single head of any of those alive, nor a single plate or cup or shoe or piece of clothing that any of then used – but I've come to know some of them and their stories quite well. I can play at being God and summon them to resurrection on the page. In my long poem *All Souls* I have assembled a named procession of one hundred of them passing through the fog at the West Gate of the town under the town clock bell that still sounds now as it did two hundred years ago. In that poem they and others cohabit with my friends and neighbours of here and now. The dead rub shoulders with those whose hearts still beat. Time's grammar is subverted as I stumble home from the pub through the town in the fog of November –

> past a meltdown of laneways and houses
> with their babies and corpses and asses and ferrets
> their pig's head and cabbage and bread and tea
> their shawls and sideboards and candlesticks

their lovers and haters and hopeless cases
their basins and kettles and Sacred Hearts
their drunkards and saviours and daughters in
    trouble
their pisspots and skillets and fishing nets
their chancers and soldiers gone to the war
their finches and dogs and darned long johns.

(from *All Souls*)

Are all narratives of history ultimately constructs of the imagination? Perhaps every truth is a partial truth and no story is the whole story. Someone has said that history tries to tell us what happened while literature tries to show how it felt. Not too long ago, a man started to tell me an anecdote; I've forgotten the details of the anecdote but I'm still marvelling at how he introduced it – 'I don't know whether or not this is true,' he said, 'but it happened.' … My own creative encounters with local historical record or evidence tend to be fortuitous in terms of turning into poems – a part of the chance of things. It is as though they seek me out, rather than the reverse.

Some stories, known or unknown, are already encoded within us, since we all carry the ghosts of other lives within our genes. My most intense and unforeseen experience of memory and the power of the written word came from the attempt to write a poem out of an unforgiveable family wound three generations back in my blood. For me, that experience belied Auden's assertion that 'Poetry makes nothing happen'. In the 1880s, my great-grandfather James Coady, an impoverished boatman on the Suir, left for America following the death of his wife, May, aged thirty-five. He left his only living child, a boy of seven, behind in Ireland, effectively abandoning him. Thirty years later, he wrote a letter from Philadelphia, pleading for forgiveness and understanding. The man who had been abandoned, my grandfather Michael Coady, dramatically burned the letter and never replied. As a boy, my father witnessed the burning and told me of it when I was a child. Years later, when I had children of my own, the unfinished story returned and troubled me into making a poem called 'The Letter'. It spoke directly to the lost father, James Coady, attempting to reply to the unanswered letter and find 'through insight and understanding' some kind of reconciliation between unquiet ghosts in my blood, three generations on.

A hundred years and I will come
to try the lane for echoes

The coughing and the crying
of children in the dark,
the nameless incarnations
of love and grief and hunger
where the river flows
coldly past.

These broken walls were witness
to your leaving, whether
in the morning sun or rain
your first-born child still sleeping
when you left him,
the dark-shawled blessings
from the doorway of a lane
you'd never see again.
...
Out of the maze of circumstance,
the ravelled tangle of effect and care,
something impelled you,
brought you finally
to bend above
the unmarked page.

An old man
in some room in Philadelphia

reaching for words to bridge
the ocean of his silence,
pleading forgiveness of the child
of Oven Lane.

(from 'The Letter')

As I wrote that poem, I still knew nothing of what
had happened in America, but the truly astonishing
fact is that, more than a century after the story began,
the published poem went out and became the catalyst
to uncover what had remained in the dark. The
poem ultimately led me to America and to my great-
grandfather's unmarked grave – a grave on which this
year I had a stone erected and from which I have taken
a handful of clay to scatter on my grandfather's grave in
Carrickbeg Friary on the slope above the river. The last
lines of the poem had proved unerringly prophetic.

Now all of these
have gone into the dark
and I would try again
to reconcile the hearts
of which my heart's compounded
with words upon a page.
I send this telling out

to meet the ghosts of its begetting,
to release it from stone mouths
of Oven Lane.

(from 'The Letter')

MÉADHBH CONWAY-PISKORSKI

Although I must declare at the outset that Méadhbh (1929–2013) was my boss in RTÉ Radio and that she and I both came from the village of Ballivor, Co. Meath, where her father was the village schoolmaster, she is included in this book as a memorable mind in her own right. Méadhbh began her working career as a teacher. She subsequently worked with the Placenames Commission before joining Children's Programmes in Radio Éireann. With the advent of the television service in 1961, she became head of Educational Programmes in RTÉ – a post she held until her retirement in 1990. Her contribution here is based on the paper she wrote for the 1993 radio series *The Tinakilly Senate*, where she argued that the Irish language is key to renewing the spirit of Ireland.

Language and Spirit

I believe our attitude to the language is fundamental in coming to grips with all the problems of our society – unemployment, alienation and the violence that comes from it in all parts of the country; it is patently an essential ingredient in our sense of being Irish, even for those who may never have learned or spoken it. The tradition of the *Gaeltachtaí* – here and in Scotland – has been an inclusive rather than an exclusive one over the centuries – as Professor Cyril Byrne of Saint Mary's University in Halifax puts it – and can encompass all the strands of our society. So I include the North in this as I reflect on the shared Gaelic tradition of all our communities. This renewal must go further than the State has gone to date. It has interpreted the ideals of Dubhghlas de hÍde [Douglas Hyde], mainly through the school system, and its actions in this domain have been successful as far as they go. But languages require much more than this for their maintenance and survival and the Irish language is even now being excluded from the restricted space it used to be given in the public arena. This trend must be reversed – not just because we should nurture it as a precious heritage as we would care for a Book of Kells – though this would be reason enough. In addition, it requires a thoroughgoing renewal if the language is to survive in the *Gaeltachtaí* and if speakers are to be encouraged and supported outside of them.

The confidence to take on this job of renewal, public recognition, public use – bringing Irish out of the closet – as a deliberate strategy to strengthen our sense of ourselves will, I believe, increase our ability to take on much more intractable difficulties that I have already mentioned – unemployment, violence, alienation.

This is the centenary year of the foundation of Conradh na Gaeilge and we recall that an Conradh was at the heart of the renewal of the spirit of Ireland at the end of the last century when there was a crisis of culture, and a need to break out of the lethargy brought about by the insidious Anglicisation of the country. The crisis today is also a cultural crisis – we have lost our sense of direction and there is a much weaker sense of who we are and where we are going. The loss of the language would be the loss of the last signpost along our journey.

Language and culture are not identical but they are very closely bound up with one another; they are the major ingredients in forming our sense of identity. Professor Joe Lee in his lively history *Ireland, 1912–1985: Politics and Society* said, 'It is hardly going too far to say that but for the loss of the language there would be little discussion about identity in the Republic. With language, little else seems to be required. Without language, only the most unusual historical circumstances suffice to develop a sense of identity.'

These unusual circumstances are beginning to disappear – he lists them as the reality or the memory of an obtrusive imperial presence, of a national revival, of a struggle for independence. As these unusual circumstances begin to fade out, 'the importance of the lost language as a distinguishing mark becomes more, not less, evident; as circumstances normalise only the hulk of identity is left without the language'. Joe Lee has put succinctly and elegantly what I certainly feel in my bones and what the vast majority of Irish people feel about the language. Time and time again in surveys, people have affirmed that Ireland would not be Ireland without its Irish-speaking people.

I wonder if you realise how hard it is to lead a full life through the Irish language – I mean to be able to use it in dealing with shops, government, at work: you ring a government department and you are likely as not to be answered in English. I usually ask for someone who can deal with me through Irish; I am asked to hold on till someone is marshalled to take the call. Now that takes some commitment of time on my part – and with the new phone charges ... Things are no better in some

County Council offices, which have a vibrant Gaeltacht to serve; one such made me feel a bit of a freak when I spoke in Irish. Few Irish speakers have the time or the persistence I have – and so after a few rebuffs they cannot be blamed for giving up, and those responsible for providing the service can then claim that there is no demand for a service in Irish.

But that is precisely how the process of Anglicisation was carried out in the first place. If I am in an Irish-speaking company and someone joins who normally does not speak Irish, the whole lot of us are expected to switch to English, even though the newcomer has enough Irish to understand what is going on. Most people who do not use Irish are not conscious of the subtle ways in which Irish can be put down – it is a mild but insidious form of ethnic cleansing.

Now this situation is unhealthy – and a symptom of a malaise with regard to identity which I have already touched on and which I will come back to. It is also a clear pointer to another characteristic of Irish society – equally distasteful. It is evidence, if more were needed, of how unfair our society really is, how arrogant the dominant groups are in asserting their all-pervasive power. Whatever our illusions may be, ours is a very undemocratic society.

Those with power act as if they had the right to put the boot in. This pervades all our attitudes – even in our dealings with children. They are rarely extended courtesy in public places; they are pushed aside in shops as if 'first come first served' could not possibly apply to them.

Women's rights had to wait an appeal to Europe. We deny some of our citizens the right to work and then resent them if we have to throw them a few crumbs. In this context, you will remember Archbishop Connell's recent warning about the subversion of the social order. We bundle together out of sight, far away from the centre of our towns and cities, those who have no property. We are content to allow division to grow between different sections of our society. We do not tolerate Travellers. We keep moving them on so that we do not have to be aware of them or deal with their existence.

As Professor [Anthony] Clare said, these evils of society only impinge on the lives of certain sections of the well-off when their house is broken into or when they witness some violent aberration. It is all of a pattern. Power not civil rights determines how any group will fare and this includes Irish speakers. They are pushed to the margins in company with other powerless groups. We have never understood the difference between controlling power – having power over – and enabling power or the power to do and allow others to do.

Our malaise and ambivalence to our *dúchas* [heritage] and to our language has many causes. It is partly a hangover from our colonial past. We learned well to despise anything that belonged to us. It is partly due to cynicism from the hypocrisy of officialdom that failed to back up the work of the schools or afford teachers basic language-teaching tools, an officialdom that seems to have covertly abandoned the language and to be bent on eliminating even its ritualistic uses.

Professor Joe Lee in the book already mentioned comments on the relationship between language and national identify. He says that 'as the struggle for independence phase draws to a close, the importance of the lost language becomes more rather than less evident'. After comparing our performance and achievements with those of smaller countries who retain their own language he concludes that 'it is provincialism of a pathetic kind to persuade ourselves that Ireland today would be necessarily a more incompetent or a more retarded society if she were Irish-speaking or bilingual rather than English-speaking'.

This provincialism is nowhere more clearly in evidence than in the use of the phrase 'an Irish solution to an Irish problem' as a term of abuse and ridicule. Surely searching for an Irish solution to an Irish problem is precisely what an independent-minded nation should be about. By confining ourselves to English, we have unconsciously accepted that what happens in England is the norm. Again, Joe Lee remarks that, if English makes certain things accessible, it closes off our access to other sources of ideas. (If something suits the English situation, given the differences of population, of history, of colonial and industrial experience, it must almost inevitably be unsuitable for us.)

An tAthair Breandán Ó Doibhlin in his essay 'Smaointe ar an Chultúr Dúchais' tells us that we had better make a conscious choice now about the Irish language. It is no longer appropriate – if it ever was – to equate our identity with Catholicism as might have happened in the past, and the Irish language is the remaining mark of identity that all can share. He says that the choice must be deliberate and based on a full knowledge of the implications of the choice for the integrity and survival of the *dúchas* or the identity.

For me, an essential part of that new *pobal* [people/ community] is the traditional solidarity between people, the fair distribution of power and wealth and the evolution of an economic and cultural order more in keeping with the reality of the needs of the 'wretched of the earth' – in the Third World and within our own shores.

Reverend Terence McCaughey in his recent book *Memory and Redemption: Church, Politics and Prophetic Theology in Ireland* quotes Peadar O'Donnell as follows: 'the roots of the present regime are not in the independence struggle but in the interests that brought about its defeat'. He then goes on to say (after referring to the Unionist establishment): 'The masters of the Dublin Establishment are less easy to identify – their addresses are multinational.'

Bord na Gaeilge in *The Irish Language in a Changing Society: Shaping the Future* puts the argument like this: 'The Irish language has played a critical role and still does in our people's sense of Irishness: it has a unique place in the continuity of our consciousness of being Irish.' It goes on to look at the problems of identity:

at the ambiguities and at the extremes of xenophobic nationalism on the one hand and on the other that would get rid of anything Irish as if it were the true mark of a modern or an international identify … This inchoate relationship to our Irishness weakens the capacity of a comparatively small society to take collective action on its problems.

It talks of 'a fractious and individualised society driven by inter-group conflicts and with few mobilising values for collective endeavour, exhibits a depleted potential for self-management; drifting increasingly towards provincialised cultural dependence and assimilation'.

Our sense of ourselves is so weak that it leaves us unable to pull together, to see that we have something worthwhile to build together – that is, the present and the future of the Irish people. The Irish language is the thread that links us to our heritage of more than a thousand years. It can supply that binding force – strong enough to bring us together and so withstand the counter-forces which are, in the end, oppressive.

Only with a secure cultural identity can we be free to think up solutions to our problems. If the reinstatement of Irish seems a daunting task, it is no more so than the task of creating full employment and no one has dared to say that that task is impossible (yes, they talk of no solution in 'the short term').

I believe as I think I heard Charles Handy say in a recent programme that the power of ideas is greater than economic theories; the secure cultural identity that a revitalised Irish language would give us could free up further our creative abilities to see our problems in a different perspective. We may need to develop 'our capacity' (as Tom Collins of Maynooth put it) 'to create our own well-being'. We may come to see that the dubious benefits of the consumer society would be a small price to pay for the deep-rooted conviviality all of us would share, from Foxrock to Foxford and from Ballymena to Ballyheigue.

I grew up with the first post-independence generation. When I was born, the Free State/Saorstát Éireann was not a decade old, but in my family there was intense joy at independence. My family was one of the many that put the Gaelic League and Griffith's Sinn Féin ideal into practice – in spite of the sadness of the recent Civil War. They felt we could walk tall with our own language now recognised, our own government, our own Gárda Síochána, our own Óglaigh na hÉireann (as I think the defence forces were then called), and our own radio station, Athlone. We had the chance to develop industries and these patriotic people supported them, in the belief that they would supply employment for all our people.

I think it was a rich heritage – it gave me what Gearóid Ó Tuathaigh calls *dhá airm aigne* – two ways of looking at the world. It enabled me to go on to learn other languages and other cultures, but, most preciously, it enabled me to appreciate *sean nós* singing, to rejoice in the richness of contemporary literature, to read Caoineadh Airt Uí Laoghaire, to mourn the passing of the McCarthys with Aogán Ó Rathaille.

JOHN COOLAHAN

Born in 1941, a native of Tarbert, Co. Kerry, John Coolahan began what would be a brilliant career in education as a primary teacher in Ballymahon, Co. Longford. He was a member of the Class of '61 and subsequently taught in Bray, Blackrock College, Carysfort College, University College Dublin and, finally, Maynooth University, where he was Professor of Education. He wrote and published extensively on Irish education and was a respected international commentator and researcher on teacher education and comparative education. He has been credited with shaping a modern vision for Irish education. On his death in 2018, the Teaching Council of Ireland described him as 'the father of Irish education'. His contribution here comes from a 1990 radio series called *Profiles from the Past* in which he examined the ideas of a number of Irish educators – in this case, Patrick Pearse.

Padraig Pearse As Educator

Education was a central concern of Padraig Pearse throughout his lifetime. This concern is reflected in his years of teaching in Westland Row CBS and University College Dublin; in his visits abroad to study the educational systems of Wales and Belgium; in his educational writing in *An Claidheamh Solais*, *An Macaomh*, *The Murder Machine*; and in many public lectures and addresses as well as in the founding and direction of his own school, St Enda's. For Pearse, educational reform was an integral aspect of the rebuilding of Irish nationhood and society which he saw as the task of his generation. On 18 April 1903, he wrote in *An Claidheamh Solais*:

> Take up the Irish problem at any point you may and you inevitably will find yourself in the end back at the education question. The prostitution of Irish education has led to many other prostitutions. Poisoned at its source the whole stream of national life has stagnated and grown foul.

Pearse was not a voice crying in the wilderness but shared in a vibrant debate and climate for educational reform. He shared two currents of thought in particular, which were having widespread contemporary impact. One was the child-centered movement which sought to focus the content and methodology of education on evolving interests, skills and aptitudes of children wherein considerable freedom for teacher and pupil would replace the imposition of rigid and formal programmes. Pearse also espoused the contemporary cultural nationalist movement which saw the schools as a means of regenerating a sense of national pride and consciousness by fostering a competence in, and love for, the Irish language, Irish history, music, songs, lore and traditions.

Pearse does not set forth a tight, rigorous, closely argued philosophy of education. In fairness, he never intended to do so. Neither is his trenchant criticism of the existing educational situation satisfactory as regards the full facts. For instance, the *Murder Machine* booklet, with its inspired pamphleteering title, largely ignores the important reforms being implemented in national schools, ignores the developments in technical education and fails to point out the initiatives for reforms which had been aired for intermediate education, which, as a system, had been eloquently condemned by the Intermediate Board itself. What Pearse was doing, and doing effectively, was campaigning to move, inspire, and enlist public interest and support for certain aspirations for which he had deep intellectual and emotional attachment. To this end he skilfully employed many rhetorical techniques, which gave a rousing thrust for radical reform and visionary zeal to his educational writings.

Several fundamental themes recur in Pearse's work. Many times he stresses the child-centered aim of education, as, for instance, 'the main object in education is to help the child to be his own true and best self' or 'the education of a child is greatly a matter, in the first place, of congenial environment and, next to this, of a wise and loving watchfulness whose chief appeal will be to the finest instincts of the child himself'.

Pearse held a very exalted view of the role/office of teacher, seeing him as an unworldly person devoted to the high vocation of fostering the growth of young people committed to his care. The teacher should bring personal enthusiasm to his work – as Pearse put it, 'so infectious an enthusiasm as shall enkindle new enthusiasm'. For Pearse, the richness of the teacher's personality and the quality of his inspiration and example were the key elements of a school. He urged greater freedom for teachers so as to deepen their professional competence and grow as people through their commitment. Pearse wanted freedom for schools to plan their educational programmes so as to suit their particular needs and circumstances rather than implement an externally devised and centrally controlled programme.

Pearse felt that existing programmes, in their neglect of Irish language and culture, denied pupils an essential part of their birthright. He wanted to restore what he termed 'the national factor' as the central focus of the curriculum. The school system which neglects this national factor, he wrote, 'commits, even from the purely pedagogic point of view, a primary blunder. It neglects one of the most powerful of educational resources.' A key area of the curriculum in which Pearse made a detailed and well-informed contribution was the promotion of bilingualism. 'In a true education,' Pearse wrote, 'religion, patriotism, literature, art and science would be brought in such a way into the daily lives of boys and girls as to affect their character and conduct.' Throughout, he urged the vitalising enrichening of the pupils by the educational material and the way it was handled.

As he looked to the future, Pearse set no small task for a Minister of Education. 'In a literal sense,' he wrote, 'the work of the first Minister of Education in a free Ireland will be a work of creation; for out of chaos he will have to evolve order and into a dead mass he will have to breathe the breath of life.' He hoped that the Minister would have an advisory council to assist him. The Department of Education would co-ordinate, maintain standards, advise, inspire and keep teachers in touch with educational research. Teachers were to have the central role in educational policy, not administrative bureaucrats. His moving vision for Irish education included 'well-trained and well-paid teachers, well-equipped and beautiful schools and a fund at the disposal of each school to enable it to award prizes on its own tests based on its own programme'. The internal organisation of schools should be democratic, with pupil involvement in school councils.

Pearse was a man who saw visions and dreamed dreams but he was also a man of action. He went on to set up an exemplar of the type of school which he hoped would become more frequent in Ireland. Having opened St Enda's at Cullenswood House, Ranelagh, in 1908, he transferred the school to the Hermitage, Rathfarnham, in 1910. A list of the characteristics of this school shows us how Pearse managed to give practical reality to his educational vision and theories. St Enda's, situated on a historic site on the slopes of the Dublin Mountains, had a splendid setting surrounded by fifty acres of fields, woodland, streams and hills. The teacher–pupil relationship fostered a humane atmosphere, with the teacher acting in the role of fosterer to the *daltaí* [students]. The mode of control was largely based on a sense of trust, an appeal to the pupils' best nature, and an involvement of pupils in the running of the school. A patriotic spirit animated the school and the legendary warrior-hero Cúchulainn was the school's inspiring model.

The formal curriculum had a most comprehensive range and balance. It included religion; Irish; English; French; German; Latin; Greek; mathematics; experimental science; history; geography; nature study; drawing; manual instruction; vocal and instrumental music; dancing; physical education; and hygiene.

However, the informal curriculum was equally impressive. A wide range of field sports were catered for while the school became famous for its drama and pageants, some of which were performed in the Abbey Theatre and Croke Park. A school museum was established and works of art adorned the school as part of an aesthetic environment. Unusual for its time, the school had a library of over two thousand volumes. School magazines were produced in which pupils participated and St Enda pupils were renowned as school debaters. The garden provided scope for practical biology and nature study. School visits to places of cultural and historic interest were a regular feature of the school year as well as lectures by distinguished visitors such as W.B. Yeats, Standish O'Grady and Douglas Hyde. Following the end of the school year, summer holiday trips to Irish-speaking districts took place. Pearse in St Enda's set an example of enlightened education policy, a live inspiration, enthusiasm and vocational commitment to his work. Both in his practical work and in his educational writings, Pearse presents a fresh radicalism which is a continuing challenge to modern Irish education.

MIKE COOLEY

Mike Cooley (1934 –2020) was born and educated in Tuam, Co. Galway. He studied engineering in Germany and later specialised in engineering design. He worked for Lucas Aerospace International in England and became a trade union activist when the company's rationalisation plan threatened to make unemployed thousands of workers who had valuable skills, experience and vision. The workers' Corporate Plan showed how their skills could be directed towards socially useful products and socially responsible systems. Mike became an international authority on human-centred technology and wrote and broadcast extensively on that theme. His best-known book is *Architect or Bee? The Human Price of Technology*. He was a regular contributor to *The Open Mind* on RTÉ Radio and gave the inaugural Open Mind Guest Lecture in 1989 on the theme 'Education for the 1990s', part of which is reproduced here. To me, his ideas are still fresh and challenging over three decades later.

Education for the 1990s

Since the fifteenth century, we have deliberately downgraded that form of work which is manual and tactile. It started at the end of the Renaissance, when academics tried to prevent master builders from using the term *magister* because it might have been confused with a Master of Arts from a university. When they found that in Alsace-Lorraine there was a tradition that, if you built twelve major structures with so many architectural elements, you'd be known as *Doctor Latimorum*; they actually tried to introduce laws to prevent this hideous development, namely, manual workers being called doctors. Yet it is precisely those manual workers who gave us the very basis of our western civilisation.

So intimidating was this embryonic, arid, academic approach that even people like Leonardo da Vinci (whom we now hold up as the pinnacle of our Renaissance person) had the following to say about these people:

They will say that not having learning, I will not speak properly of that which I wish to elucidate, but do they not know that my subjects are the better illustrated from experience, than by yet more words: experience, which has been the mistress of all those who wrote well, and thus as mistress, I will cite her in all cases.

The great Dürer, known to most people as an artist, was also a great professor of mathematics. He actually pointed out that it would be possible to develop new forms of mathematics, which, as he put it, would be as amenable to the human spirit as natural language. He was talking about a very different form of learning and understanding. We need forms which allow us to interact closely with nature and learn from nature. I learned so much about aerodynamics by watching trees in motion. My early insight into guidance systems was when I wondered how the geese used to come to the west of Ireland about this time each year – the third week in October – and how they had guided themselves from Canada and Siberia.

There was a sense in which one could see the greatness of nature, and one began to understand that we had to accord with it. I think people used to say, 'Ní hé lá na gaoithe lá na scolb', which means that you actually mould what you're doing partly to accord with nature. It is most important as we move towards the 1990s that we look at other cultures and other ways of viewing these relationships. There's the great saying from the North American Indian when his people were being rounded up in the compound:

I say to you my people, the paleface will take the eagle from the sky, he will take the salmon from the streams, he'll take the buffalo from the plains, he'll poison the air that we breathe and the water that we drink.

That was much more accurate a prediction than the Hudson Institute was able to do even ten years ago, because he saw precisely what it was we were doing to nature and to ourselves. I can't imagine that, if one had that relationship and concern with nature, one could contemplate, as apparently is now the case, that fertiliser will be poured on the Burren in the west of Ireland.

It is going to be essential in the 1990s to develop forms of education which do not confuse linguistic ability with intelligence. I'm not talking here about the capacity to tell stories or be descriptive – I hold that to be a marvellous attribute. I'm talking about that narrow point of view, the belief that unless you can write a great thesis about something, you don't actually understand it. Most people I know express their intelligence by what they do and how they do it, rather than the way they write and talk about it. I saw at Lucas Aerospace that incredible creativity and energy of people if a framework was set up which allowed them to use their talents in that sort of way.

It is going to be essential that we end the division between young and old people. It is already predicted, in Britain in any case, that 80 per cent of all those who will be working in commerce and industry in the next century are already there. There are terrific demographic shifts taking place which will require educational forms that allow people to continue to develop right through their lives – that you just don't switch off at fifty.

In that sense, I think the Greeks had it absolutely correct when they used to suggest 'how dull it is to pause, to make an end, to rust unburnished, not to shine in use'. There is a wealth of talent amongst people that could be marshalled to deal with the problems of our society; vast packages of knowledge which could be handed on to future generations.

It is going to be essential in the 1990s in the field of science and technology that we create environments in which more women will come into science and technology – not as imitation men or as honorary males or grotesque Margaret Thatcher-like figures – but with the courage to question the male value system, which, in my view, has dominated Western science and technology for too long.

We should create joint courses where people can study both science and arts together. I worked for a long time on a very interesting computer system which works out a transformation from data to information, from information to knowledge, knowledge to wisdom, wisdom to action. It is a kind of cybernetic loop which is now being researched at the University of Tokyo. I was quite proud about this little invention of mine until one of my colleagues said, 'I'm sure I saw something like that in a poem by T.S. Eliot.' And sure enough, I got out the *Collected Works* and there was a poem which concluded by saying:

Where is the wisdom we have lost in knowledge?
Where is the knowledge we have lost in
    information?

So often artists and writers and poets will prefigure the big issues in society, and we do ourselves great damage as engineers and scientists if we separate ourselves from that.

Above all else, it is going to be necessary to kindle a sense of imagination and excitement. When you say that, people will say, 'Well, that may be alright in music or in literature,' but you look at what the great scientists have to say. The great Einstein said, 'Imagination is far more important than knowledge.' And he went on to say:

> The mere formulation of a problem is far more important than its solution, which might be merely a matter of experimental or mathematical skill. To raise new problems, to look at old problems from a new aspect, marks the real advances in science.

When he was being pressed by one of these arid reductionists at MIT [Massachusetts Institute of Technology] to say how it was that he arrived at the Theory of Relativity, they would have loved if he agreed that it was some narrow mathematical regression, where you squeezed out the only answer in a regression which led you to the one best way. Einstein horrified them, apparently, by suddenly saying, 'When I was a child of fourteen, I asked myself what it might be like to ride on a beam of light and look back at the world.' A beautiful conceptual framework to which he subsequently provided the mathematics.

It is going to require a lot of courage to face up to these issues because we have been so dominated by this reductionist type of thinking that it will require great personal courage, and people perhaps sacrificing their careers, to question these issues. Nations as a whole will have to show their courage. I find it extraordinary that a nation which had the courage to stand up for eight hundred years to an apparently implacable enemy – British imperialism – at a time when there was hardly a crack in its edifice, and was able, generation after generation, to produce people who asserted the right to nationhood and to its culture, now seems to be so disoriented and so apathetic about the situation which faces it.

Above all else, it seems to me, it is going to be necessary to look at the skills and interests of people, to build on the positive things about human beings. There is an awful characteristic, which is common also in Ireland, to look at people's weaknesses. The very basis of our examinations is to find out what people *don't* know, rather than what they *do* know. People laugh when they hear of the tradition that used to be at Cambridge which is: if you got a question you didn't like, you just ignored it and wrote your own question. That really is what life is about – writing your own questions and answering them in a profound way. That's what people do when they do an MA or a PhD. I think this terrible emphasis on what people don't know, this destructiveness, putting people down, was most powerfully expressed by James Joyce in *Finnegans Wake*, where he described the two characters in any human being, Shem and Shaun, and he warned us of the danger of concentrating on the negative character:

> Sniffer of carrion, premature gravedigger, seeker of the nest of evil in the bosom of a good word, you who sleep at our vigil and fast for our feast, you with your dislocated reason [...] you have reared your disunited kingdom on the vacuum of your own most intensely doubtful soul.

I think we have to transcend our 'doubtful souls' and be willing to question some of these issues I have described.

JAMES DEENY

James Deeny (1906–1994) was born in Lurgan, Co. Armagh, the son of a local GP. He was educated by the Jesuits in Clongowes Wood College, Co. Kildare, and qualified as a doctor at Queen's University Belfast at the age of twenty-one. He joined his father's practice and continued his postgraduate studies, acquiring further academic honours within a short time.

James Deeny's work with the poor country people in Co. Armagh influenced much of his later innovative work, particularly the Mother and Child Scheme and research on tuberculosis. In 1944, he was appointed chief medical officer to the then Department of Local Government and Public Health in Dublin. With a handful of other devoted public servants, he was the architect of much of Ireland's health legislation. He conducted a national tuberculosis survey from 1950 to 1953.

Subsequently, he had a distinguished career with the World Health Organization and as scientific adviser to the Holy See. In retirement, further careers involved farming and community development. He published his memoir *To Cure and To Care: Memoirs of a Chief Medical Officer* in 1989. His contribution here is based on his *My Education* interview in 1990 and on material from *To Cure and To Care*, a radio series based on his memoir.

A Life in Medicine

My preparation for medicine was very funny. I said to my father one day, 'I'm fed up with school. If I can pass my "matric", can I start medicine?' So I sat the matric [matriculation examination] at Queen's when I was sixteen. I was actually in medical school in my sixteenth year and I qualified at twenty-one. You could do that in those days. Really, my father had taught me my medicine, although I was very well taught at Queen's. Queen's was a very bigoted place, but naturally you became the best of friends with the others in the class. There were only two Catholics on the staff of Queen's, right down to the cleaners, and yet I got a first-class training; there was never any difference made. You could still win a prize, but on the other hand, you never had a hope of getting on the staff.

I started hanging around the laboratories in Queen's and there were two or three remarkable men there. Dickie Hunter, who was the secretary of the university and a lecturer in anatomy, became a great friend of mine. He taught me all sorts of little things about research and anatomy. Eventually, I got my nose into bacteriology and I gradually worked my way in there. This gave me an interest in laboratory work and research.

I went into my father's practice in Lurgan. Again, my father taught me many skills, like how to pull teeth. In those days, there was no free dental service and old people didn't have the money. An old man would come and say, 'Dr Jim, could you pull that tooth?' I would get my father's forceps and jack it out, but I would freeze it first so he wouldn't feel it. During the hungry '30s, people got a bit of dole and there was a bit of outdoor relief, but eventually they would be cut off and people were literally faced with starvation. The Vincent de Paul Society did their best and there was also an organisation called the Ladies of Charity, but it was all pretty ineffectual.

I was taught by the people of Lurgan. I had my eyes opened, coming from a posh school down the south and then coming home and living and working with these people. If you delivered a mother's first baby, you were her friend for life. You became part of the family. We always earned money, but for weeks during the really bad times I never saw a fee. They hadn't got it and you didn't ask them for it. When the war came and people got work and there was money floating around, every one of those people came and paid me. When I left Lurgan, there was very little bad debt – they all came and paid you when they had it and, when they hadn't it, you minded them and there was no nonsense about it. You had a responsibility.

Every year I wrote a research paper. It was very simple research, but I was on the ball with it. I discovered the 'blue men' (a diet deficiency) and, within three days, I turned a man pink who had been 'blue' for thirty years. I became world-famous for about a week! Eventually, I came to Dublin as chief medical adviser to the Department of Health. One of the extraordinary things about Ireland has been the integrity and quality of the senior civil servants in this country. I have seen the inside of fourteen governments all over the world and I have seen crookery and knavery, but the senior civil servants that I worked with – and not only the medical fellows – like J.D. McCormack, [Theo] McWeeney and [Des] Hourihane, were all outstanding people.

This country is blessed in the people it has in the civil service. Look at the Hospitals' Sweepstake money. They spent hundreds of millions of pounds building hospitals and not one penny of that money went astray. There is no other country that could do that. I was very young relative to these people and one of the things I came to respect was their judgement, their wisdom, in the old-fashioned sense of the word. These men had all worked their way up in the civil service in different ways. Some of them had been in prison or had been condemned to death because they had fought for their country. Others had simply worked their way through the county councils and so on. They taught me to stop and look, stop and think, be careful what you say and then stand up and say something unpopular if you know it to be right. I was a mere general practitioner when I was brought in there.

Later on, I went off to work with the World Health Organization, which was a wonderful experience. I was chief of the mission in Indonesia and did national TB [tuberculosis] surveys in Sri Lanka and Somaliland.

I love art. I have seen all the great art exhibitions in Europe because, when I was sent to a conference, I would get up early in the morning in order to visit them. I always made sure that I saw anything worth visiting.

When I was a medical student, I used to travel up and down from Lurgan to Queen's every day. There was a bookshop beside the station and, if I had half an hour to wait for my train, I would poke through the books. One day, I bought a wee book called *Simplicity* by Pastor Valmer. His belief was that you should make your life simple and not complicate it with possessions – don't complicate life by riding one hundred horses at once! He was echoing a medieval scholastic, William of Occam, a Franciscan from England whose philosophy came to be known as 'Occam's Razor' – one cuts away all the extraneous things in any philosophical hypothesis to bring it down to one central thought. I followed this idea in my research. If I had a job to do, I did just that and cut out all other distractions. It is like those people who want to write a novel but never do because they have too many other irons in the fire. If you want to write a novel, you get on and write it. There were many other suggestions in this book. For instance, if something is very, very important, you do it immediately. Another theme was prevention, which became central to me throughout my medical career – so much disease is preventable. A final theme was simplicity.

I developed a great interest in the old Irish monks, way back in the Golden Age of Ireland, and, wherever

I went in Europe, I used to look for their history. It was a very emotional experience, to visit somewhere like the library of St Gall in Switzerland and see all the old Irish manuscripts, beautifully illuminated. I would imagine some poor character starting off in Clonmacnoise or Durrow or Bangor with the same book in a leather satchel on his back and carrying a staff and wearing an old wool habit, crossing seas and marshes, being attacked, starving and sick and, eventually, reaching one of the great monasteries that had been founded by the Irish, like St Gall. Imagining all that, it is then incredible to see the actual book, eight or nine hundred years later. Three years ago, when I was eighty, I went out to Skellig Michael and climbed the Skellig. It frightened the wits out of me! But such places have inspired me. In one way it is their austerity but, in another way, the Irishness in me makes me glory in what these men achieved.

Eventually, I came down here to Wexford and got very much involved in the whole idea of community development. The ordinary people of an area like Tagoat or Rosslare have educated me greatly. I meet more brains in the course of a day than you would in a university and an awful lot of them never had a chance in life. Some of them have a contentment, they are perfectly happy at what they are doing. There are a lot of people in a place like Tagoat who are content and wise and this is a very good thing. Everywhere, even right under your feet, there is something to be learned, something to be done, and this is the important thing about community development. I have been educated by wonderful men like Pat Stafford and Lar Doyle, and ladies like Jenny O'Brien and Mary Murphy. They have taught me goodness – there is an awful lot of good in people. Once you start community development, it brings out the creativity in people. Our education system smothers creativity, but we need to bring it out in people.

In my life, I have had some good periods and some not so good, but the years I spent with the National Tuberculosis Survey were amongst the best. We were fortunate in having two brilliant radiologists, Niall Walsh first, who developed the mass radiography techniques with Ann Roddy and the other radiographers. When he left to go to Newfoundland, Joan MacCarthy joined us. The total cost of the survey was £50,000.

I had some fantastic luck. If I had not attended the 6th International Congress of Radiology in London in July 1950 (just after commencing the survey), the first such congress for nearly fifteen years, I would not have seen the first ever mirror-camera mass X-ray unit shown by Elema-Schonander of Sweden. Then, with the advice and encouragement of some Irish radiologists who were present, I bought the set off the manufacturers' stand, brought it home, and so had the first mirror-camera unit in these islands.

We started a development programme under Niall Walsh and Ann Roddy, with training and handling exercises, and, when we had learnt enough, I had the set mounted on a Bedford truck, with a body which we designed and had built in Dublin. We refined it down so that the unit could go anywhere and be operated with one radiographer and a driver/technician and could be plugged into any 15 amp light socket, or might be stopped and used at any crossroads or in any small schoolhouse. This was essential and ideal for our scattered rural population. When we finished our R&D [research and development] work, we wrote it up and published it in *Tubercle: The Journal of the British Tuberculosis Association*. It aroused a lot of interest as it was the first account of the first mirror-camera unit in Great Britain or Ireland. The successful development of mass radiography in this country was based on this work.

One of the most important things done in tuberculosis was to set up the National Report Centre. Some sort of feedback was essential, to enable us to monitor what we were doing and how well we were doing it. So we established a unit in Dublin Corporation Tuberculosis Department under Dr Gallen and organised it so that every new case of tuberculosis occurring in the country was reported to this centre. Dr Gallen worked closely with Dr Michael Daly, who looked after TB on the medical side of the department.

In 1958, I was coming home with Michael Daly from some TB affair or other and I turned to him and said, in a smug, pompous way, 'Do you know, Michael, I am finally satisfied that we have a really first-class TB service.' He agreed, with equal self-satisfaction. The next morning, he came into my office and said that Colm Gallen had been on the phone and that the number of new cases reported, which we knew to be dropping fast, had gone so far that the previous month there had not been a single new case reported for the whole country. At the time, we really did not pay too much attention to this, feeling that it was a one-off occurrence.

The following month, Dr Gallen came in himself to my office in the Custom House and told us that there had been no new case for the second month running. This in spite of the whole paraphernalia of mass radiography, the general practitioners, hospital outpatients; the lot all busy at work looking for cases. We sat there and looked at one another. It took quite a while to sink in. Here was the tuberculosis epidemic, which had lasted for more than a hundred years and which had killed more than three-quarters of a million Irish men, women and children and on which we had been working for years, finally coming to an end. So far as I remember, we shook hands but otherwise were in a kind of daze. There were no victory celebrations or parades; I don't think we even went out for a drink to celebrate this amazing achievement. Of course, we realised that the danger was still there and would return if we were not on our guard.

PATRICIA DONLON

Patricia Donlon was born in Dublin in 1943 and has had a distinguished career in books and art, having been director of both the Chester Beatty Library and the National Library of Ireland. She was also director of the Tyrone Guthrie Centre in Annaghmakerrig, Co. Monaghan. She is a respected authority on children's books and in that capacity was a core contributor to the radio series *Children Reading* – an eight-part guide for parents to the world of children's books. She also gave the final Open Mind Guest Lecture in 2002, in which she spoke of her lifetime involvement with children's books. Her contribution here, however, is based on her programme in the radio series *My Millennium*, where she gave her personal perspective on life in the second millennium.

A Fair Field, Full of Folk

Thinking about a millennium requires an awful lot of work so rather than attempt to review it chronologically, I would rather look on it as a large mosaic or tapestry. I think particularly of the medieval poet, William Langland, and his poem *Piers Plowman* when 'In a summer season when soft was the sun', dressed in a shepherd's robe he 'had a vision of a fair field'. These were 'a fair field full of folk [...]/Of all manner of men, the rich and the poor'.

This is my vision – a fair field full of folk: individuals (men and women) who make up this tapestry and left their mark on the millennium just ended. To the fore would be Hildegard of Bingen (1098–1179), a most remarkable woman. When she was just eight, she was sent to a convent as a tithe to the Church, where she spent her early years as a spiritual companion to an abbess and together they formed an abbey. She was a manager, a visionary, a poet, a composer, a writer on medicines and cures and on botany. Her music is extraordinary and I think it's rather wonderful that here, at the beginning of this new millennium, we can listen to the spiritual soaring of her songs. Yes she was a mystic but in the abbey they wore jewellery and bright clothes – most unconventional for nuns of that time!

Keeping in that spirit and moving across the tapestry, I would love to be in the company of Chaucer and his pilgrims telling their tales on the way to Canterbury. These were tough times – a lot of pestilence and wars – but there was also a lot of laughter. The humour of these pilgrims has translated across the centuries and different languages. I would love to have been in the company of Chaucer, the knight, the miller and so on. I might then move to another great medieval site – Santiago de Compostela – as Chaucer reminds us that one of his pilgrims was always boasting of how she had been to 'St James'. People went on these pilgrimages for a variety of reasons – penitential and spiritual – so I think it would be quite extraordinary to go there too. And now that I'm in Spain, I'm moving on to the sixteenth century to meet another extraordinary woman, another mystic, St Teresa of Ávila. Also like Hildegard, she was a great manager – feisty, funny and down to earth. She has left us her memoirs and letters. I think I would be very comfortable with her. She was very holy but not pious. It is said she would scold God for her levitating while in the middle of preparing dinner! I would also love to have met El Cid while we're in Spain – probably the equivalent of today's pop hero! – who rode out against the Moors in defence of the Christians. Another legendary hero.

I'm talking here in my little book room surrounded by the many books that have given me such pleasure over the years and they remind me of probably the greatest invention of the millennium – Gutenberg's printing press. Despite all the advances in technology, it is still the most remarkable and impactful invention. Before Gutenberg, the process of making a book was so laborious and tedious and costly and, even then, it belonged to a community. There was no such thing as a personally owned book. Suddenly, with this invention, the notion that you could have thousands of copies of exactly the same text to send out across the world – it really was revolutionary. Here in this room I am surrounded by so many friends, so many great minds and intellects of the millennium. I can know what they thought and how they lived for a very small price. The internet is a wonderful concept but so much of it is book-based.

Again, in terms of its effect on my own life, the invention of recorded voices and music and ultimately radio was quite extraordinary. In the comfort of my room or my car I can sit and hear great voices, great music, ideas being discussed, stories being told. I remember as a child the magic of radio which led me into those worlds. Think of the legacy that someone like Shakespeare has left us – another major figure in my tapestry. I was delighted that he was voted man of the millennium in Britain. All of human life and human emotions are in his work and thanks to the printing press and recorded sound his texts are with us today – as fresh and vital as ever. I think of Shakespeare's lovely song,

Where the bee sucks, there suck I
In a cowslip's bell I lie

[*Tempest*, Act V, Scene I]

and I am reminded of how much we have lost in nature – whole species of plants and animals – the cowslip and the bumblebee are among those under threat.

I recognise that, in the wide canvas of a millennium, there were many dark periods. Langland's poem did include 'all manner of men/the rich and the poor'. Going back to Spain, there was the Inquisition – a reign of terror, done in the name of religion. More recently, inhumanities such as the Holocaust remind us of the sheer evil the world has witnessed.

For children, the millennium has brought dramatic change. At the beginning of the millennium, children were looked on as miniature adults and child mortality was extremely high. But children had brighter moments, too. In the Chester Beatty Library there is a medieval manuscript of a Book of Hours which depicts children at play with hoops, balls, skipping ropes, etc. Children will always play. They are by nature happy beings. The danger today is that in ordering and structuring their lives, we are threatening to rob them of playtime in its most natural form, letting their imagination have free rein – just being able to 'mullock' around, doing 'nothing' as some adults would put it. I worry too about the loss of street games and nursery rhymes which are part of an inheritance stretching back to medieval times.

On the plus side, children's books have brought a whole new world of magic and wonder to the world of little people. The advent of colour printing at the end of the nineteenth century was a major boon. A favourite artist of mine is Rosamond Praeger, [Robert] Lloyd Praeger's sister, who produced a range of magical and funny picture books, the forerunner of so many wonderful artists who delight today's children. Today we have tremendous artists producing amazing picture books for children. A child today may be six, seven, eight before they are inside an art gallery to view a painting, but in the books in our bookshops and libraries they can see some of the most amazing art between the covers of a children's book.

From my time in the National Library, I am greatly aware of how photography has contributed to our understanding of the past. There is something extraordinary in how old photographs can capture the essence and spirit of my ancestors living their lives. I can fully sympathise with primitive peoples who were frightened of the camera because they thought when you captured their image, you captured their soul. My children and grandchildren will be able to hold an image of their ancestors and know what they looked like, where they lived and what they wore. We have a remarkable collection of photographs of Irish life over the past century and more to remind us of the old adage that one picture is worth a thousand words. Film, of course, was the most extraordinary medium of the twentieth century and its development brought the world into our living rooms.

I began with music from the beginning of the millennium. May I conclude with music from the end of that great span of years? I love the music of Hoagy Carmichael. The lyrics of 'Ole Buttermilk Sky', 'Georgia on My Mind' and 'Washboard Blues' resonate with me and epitomise to a degree the glamour of the American life that we saw in comics, in *The Saturday Evening Post* and in the movies. The relaxed and easy sound of his music is just magic and marvellous for me. If I could take someone from my 'fair field of folk' out to dinner I would definitely opt for Hoagy Carmichael!

DENIS DONOGHUE

Although he was born in Tullow, Co. Carlow, Denis Donoghue (1928–2021) was reared from a very early age in Warrenpoint, Co. Down, where his father was a sergeant in the RUC (Royal Ulster Constabulary). He became one of the world's foremost scholars of modern literature, holding professorships in University College Dublin (his alma mater) and New York University. He wrote over thirty books, including definitive studies of W.B. Yeats, Jonathan Swift and Emily Dickinson. He had a wonderful command of the English language as a lecturer. One student recalled that 'it was easy to mistake his grand rolling cadences for the voice of God'. In this excerpt from his 1992 *My Education* interview, he has little regard for his formal schooling. It was largely outside influences – a neighbour's library and latterly the National Library in Dublin – that shaped the young scholar.

My Real Education

I went to the local Catholic school, St Peter's, a small three-teacher school. One of the teachers, Sean Crawford, a rather remarkable and genial character, lived a few doors from us, just in the square. We had the run of the Crawfords' house. I formed with him and his daughter a little trio and we used to play music. Even more to the point, he was a literary person who made available to me his small but fairly select library. In my family we had no books at all of the slightest significance. Apart from schoolbooks, I recall only one book in the house and that was a book my father had, called *A Guide to Careers*, which indeed was a very useful book. When I wanted something to read, I would go through Sean Crawford's collection of books, so the beginnings of my readings were done with the aid of his library. It had the standard works of English fiction – Jane Austen, George Eliot and so on. There was a magazine at the time called *John O'London's Weekly* and he had a very large bound volume, an entire year's issue. I think what first started my interest in literary criticism was this bound volume, because, in addition to stories, it had several critical essays by people like Robert Lynd and Frank Swinnerton, who were men of letters at the time.

I got my first introduction to what it was to write a formal essay and perhaps even to have it published through *John O'London's Weekly*, because these were civilised English essays that had a beginning, a middle and an end, in that order.

Sean Crawford used to write little essays and little squibs for *The Irish Press*. He was a strange, angular and rather daft individual, but extraordinarily humane. I remember him vividly as a teacher, not in terms of anything very tangible he taught me, but in the sense that he really made it clear to me that there was a larger world out there that was full of all kinds of magical things: novels and poems and music.

I was largely self-taught at that stage. No one told me what the difference was between good writing and bad writing. I kept lists and I would write down words which struck me as interesting or words that I came across in my reading which were unfamiliar to me. It was, in some ways, a forerunner of my situation when I came to Dublin and I would steal the book dockets from the National Library so that I wouldn't have to buy jotters. I would come across a sentence that struck me as memorable and write it down and commit it to memory. I began in Warrenpoint by simply writing down single words, words which struck me as either having some resonance or some interesting meaning. When I tried to write an essay, I used some of these words, morally disreputable and pretentious, of course. In the same way, when I became a university student, I would try to work these flashy quotations into my formal essays to dazzle my teachers.

Eventually, I moved from St Peter's into the secondary school, which was the Christian Brothers' school, the Abbey CBS, in Newry. That wasn't a place of very happy memories. One of my great difficulties there was that I was preceded by my elder brother, Tim. He certainly was not a hard-working student, but he was something far more important in the school at the time – a great footballer. He played Gaelic football for the inter-provincial team and I have to say that he was by far the most intelligent Gaelic footballer I've ever seen. Tim played Gaelic football in the way in which the young George Best played soccer. His career came to a very sudden end because he did a very foolish thing. Instead of preserving his body for the purposes of college football, which was relatively civilised, he played in the local Warrenpoint team against Mayo Bridge and various other Gaelic football teams and, eventually and predictably, had the cartilage smashed in his right knee and never played again. Brother Newell, who was besotted with Gaelic football, regarded Tim as a hero and I was of no account at all, because of my absolute indifference to all sport, and most particularly to Gaelic football. So my days in the CBS were very much darkened by my complete contempt for all sport and, in that sense, my years there weren't very happy.

I was taught English very badly. It was merely a matter of memorising ostensibly critical observations: if we were talking about romantic poetry, we should bring in the following seven points and so on – a fairly deadening exercise. It was never explained what literature was about or why it existed or what the imagination was or what was the difference between transcribing an event and imagining one. There was no indication that literature was anything but material you learned by heart – a poem was just something that didn't hit the margins of the page. There was no sense of literature itself, as distinct from history or geography.

My favourite subject was Latin. I admired its composure, the way in which the words were placed, the movement of the sentence. I was taught very well by a remarkable teacher, Pádraic Crinion. His way of teaching us Latin was not to simply go through Latin grammar but to start with Cicero's letters, thereby learning the grammar by reading Cicero – a very daring thing in certain respects but quite wonderful as a method. We weren't just chanting phrases and rules of grammar; we saw what Cicero was doing in the speeches and we saw that there was a relation between the grammar, the syntax and the rhetoric of the speech and how it was persuasive. I learned an immense amount of Latin from that and also a sense of a different culture.

When my father retired from the police in September 1946, we all drifted in different directions. I went to Dublin and my father and mother went down to Tullow, where there was a house available. My first inclination was to study law. I saw myself as a barrister and it took me about a week to discover that there was no question of that. My father couldn't possibly have afforded all the King's Inns nonsense – the dinners and the fees and so on. Very reluctantly, I switched to a degree in arts.

At that time, we did five subjects in UCD [University College Dublin] in the first year and my five were Latin, English, Irish, history and mathematics. Latin and English were the major subjects I wanted to concentrate on, but it was still a sadness to me that I was unable to do law. I have a strange reverence for law and for the verbal precision, the majesty of it. I always read law reports with great interest and I like their finesse and delicacy. I like talking to lawyers. I like having a conversation with someone who is a trained lawyer, someone who is trained in the niceties of the law, not just in the sprawl of human life. I like that sense of there being order and precision, even though living may be a much more chaotic business.

I didn't really enjoy college life. Even by Irish standards at the time, I was very impoverished. I resented the fact that, for instance, medical students who were my immediate colleagues were far better dressed and lived in fancy houses in Foxrock or Stillorgan, while I was living in miserable digs on the South Circular Road. So, at a very early stage, I shifted my centre of gravity from UCD in Earlsfort Terrace to the Royal Irish Academy of Music in Westland Row. I was very lucky to be able to lead a kind of double life in Dublin. I was far happier in the Royal Irish Academy of Music than I was in Earlsfort Terrace. It wasn't that I despised the teachers or the lecturers – I recognised, for instance, that the late Jerry Hogan was an immensely learned and civilised person – but I did most of my reading and studying in the National Library. They were the good old days when the National Library was open from ten o'clock in the morning until ten o'clock at night. I read omnivorously and took copious notes and also acquired a kind of low cunning in manipulating other people's ideas.

The great writer during my time growing up was T.S. Eliot. I managed to arrange a couple of meetings with him in London and he was my hero. He was for me a great writer, a great poet, a great critic. At a very early age, I started getting in touch with American writers and critics, major figures like Kenneth Burke, John Crowe Ransom, R.P. Blackmur. These were the people I revered and, indeed, still do, so that I was oriented much more towards America than Cambridge, where I was living and teaching. I was becoming very Americanised. I was reading a lot of American literature and American poets, so that American criticism and scholarship meant more to me then than English criticism and scholarship.

ANNE FINE

Anne Fine (*b*. 1947) is a writer who lives in Durham, England. She writes for both adults (*Madame Doubtfire*) and children (*Bill's New Frock*; *Flour Babies*). Many of her children's books have won awards and have made her one of the most popular authors of children's fiction writing today. She gave the Open Mind Guest Lecture on RTÉ Radio in 1996, when she enthralled the audience with her humour and her insight into the world of children's books. She was the UK's Children's Laureate from 2001 to 2003. Her contribution here is taken from an *Open Mind* interview in December 2000.

Children and Books
Children read for many reasons. One of them is enchantment. Generally, if they are not enchanted by a book, it won't work. No child has ever come up to me

and said, 'I loved your book' – *Goggle-Eyes* or *Flour Babies* or whatever – 'but I haven't had time to finish it, because I don't find much time to read.' That is why children read as they walk to the bus-stop, as they sit on the lavatory, as they eat their toast and marmalade. Of course, there are different types of enchantment. Sometimes as adults we are disquieted when we look at the covers of books our children are reading, but children can be turned on by an extraordinary range of literature. I had a letter from an eight-year-old who said, 'I've just read your book *A Sudden Swirl of Icy Wind* (which I think is quite a sweet book). Some of my other favourite books are *Street Fighter II*, *The Pizza Monster* and *Bambi*.' Here is clearly a very eclectic reader!

I write mostly about families. I like to write about families under pressure, because they are most interesting. As someone said, 'Happiness writes white.' If you write about a family where everybody is happy and everything is hunky-dory, it is going to be boring. So I tend to write about families under stress; families breaking up. I don't make the books gloomy but I do make them realistic and I am well known for taking quite difficult subjects and writing them with a fair level of humour.

An important aspect of writing for children is that they can have a character whom they can identify with. That character may not be like you but he or she may be how you would like to be and the child reader will respond to that. Empathy is so important to the reader. Children do not easily talk in abstracts but if you give them a book it's as if you have given them a moral template against which they can say things they are confident with, like 'I would have spoken up sooner' or 'I would not have dared to do that.' There's a lovely quote by Lionel Trilling in an essay on education: 'The purpose of a humanistic education was to read about the conduct of other people as presented by a writer highly endowed with moral imagination and to see this conduct as relevant to our own, in that it redeems the individual from moral torpor.'

Reading can also give the child a sense of empowerment. The world is a rather peculiar place and the novel embodies a sort of truth about the world. It is the author's truth. A child who senses that the world is one particular way may find that their teacher won't admit it, their parents won't admit it but often the author can admit it because they have the licence of it being fiction. It can be very gratifying for an author to sense in a child's letter that you have triggered something that is emotionally important to them. Boys in particular can be so outspoken and honest in writing about family matters. It's very difficult to write emotional lies. The truth will break out and I get letters of such emotional depth from children, which makes me feel I have done something important for some children. I have written the book they needed to read at that time.

A book can be analysed to death in the classroom by some teachers. It's better to stay clear of some of the unimaginative, even leaden, approaches that are pursued in classrooms. Why have they chosen ME to torture the children with? I suppose the occasional book has to be trodden all over and lay down its life for a greater higher purpose. If anyone ever bought me a ticket for *A Midsummer Night's Dream*, I would probably try and choke them with it, because I never ever want to have anything to do with it again. We studied it for a year at school and I hated it, but the fact is that because of some of the work we did on it, I can make sense of all of Shakespeare's plays now in a way that has given me pleasure all through my reading life. I will go to anything else – but not *A Midsummer Night's Dream*. And, in fairness, I also get letters which show that teachers have done inspired work with books of mine. Teachers and children clearly enjoyed themselves and that's hugely gratifying for me as an author.

GERRY FITT

Gerry Fitt (1926–2005) was born in Belfast and grew up amid the severe unemployment and poverty of the 1930s. When he was nine, his father died of tuberculosis. This placed an extreme burden on his mother and, to help alleviate the situation, Gerry went to work after leaving school. He later went to sea and spent the war years working on ships. In the 1950s, he was drawn into politics and was initially elected as a city councillor, before finally making the breakthrough as a Member of Parliament in 1965. At all levels of politics, he has been a non-sectarian representative. In 1968, he was prominently involved in the emerging civil rights movement and, when people like John Hume, Ivan Cooper and Paddy Devlin were subsequently elected to parliament, Gerry Fitt joined, reluctantly, with them and others, to form the Social Democratic and Labour Party.

In the ill-fated Sunningdale Executive, Gerry Fitt was appointed deputy chief executive of the Northern Ireland Executive, after the Sunningdale Agreement. He was always an outspoken critic of the IRA and was often attacked for his stance. In 1979, he left the SDLP and, in 1983, narrowly lost his West Belfast seat. Shortly afterwards, his house was burned out and he moved to London. He was created Lord Fitt in 1983 but, as far as Northern Ireland is concerned, he will 'always be there'. His contribution here is based on his 1991 interview for the series *My Education*.

A Life in Politics

I was born on 9 April 1926 and Paisley was born on 6 April so the two of us were born in the one week. My mother used to say that the devil was busy that week! One of my very earliest political memories was, when I was about seven, coming home from chapel and a fellow giving me a leaflet. I couldn't read it very well at that age, but I kept it for years and years. It was a quotation from James Connolly and it has played a great part in my political thinking.

Ireland apart from her people means nothing to me. The man who is full of love and enthusiasm for Ireland and can yet walk through her streets unmoved and witness all the wrong and suffering, shame and degradation that is wrought upon the people of Ireland by Irish men and Irish women without burning in his heart to end this wrong is, in my opinion, a sham, a liar and a cheat, no matter how much he may profess to love that combination of chemical elements which he is pleased to call Ireland.

It was the people of Ireland that Connolly was concerned with and it is the people of Ireland that I have been concerned with.

My father, who was very ill at the time, had been involved in the labour movement in Ireland. He worked in Gallagher's tobacco factory, but he died in 1935 when I was very young. I lived in a Catholic ghetto beside the New Lodge Road, where we felt very hemmed in. We never thought about it, but we began to develop a big boulder on our shoulders: we were second-class citizens. There was massive unemployment in the area; lots of people were living on what they then called 'Outdoor Relief'. When my father died, there were six of us left, three boys and three girls. My mother had to go out every day to work as a domestic. I think she was paid two shillings a day. I used to meet her coming home. I remember vividly how tired she used to be.

I was thirteen when the war began. When I turned fourteen, I got a job in a barber shop and earned five shillings a week. In 1941, I went away to sea, down in the bowels of the ship shovelling coal. My brother-in-law and my brother were the other two firemen, so they did the heavy bits.

I met my wife at Hyde Park Corner, in 1947, a wee girl from Castlederg. We were married in November of the same year. I didn't want to go to sea after I met Ann, so I came home. In 1949, a very nasty election took place in Northern Ireland. The whole partition issue came very much to the fore. The Anti-Partition League decided that they would fight every seat in Northern Ireland. They had collections outside churches after Mass all over the Republic, so the Unionists sneeringly referred to it as the 'Chapel Gate Election'. I came home just before the end of the election and I got involved in a minor way. A by-election was called for October 1951 and Jack Beattie was a Labour candidate. That was when the political bug bit me, and it's been with me ever since. I went out campaigning for Jack Beattie.

I starved myself, I didn't want anything at all, I just wanted to see him elected. We fought the election tooth and nail and, after five recounts, Jack Beattie won by twenty-five votes. It was a very emotional time for me and, as soon as he was declared elected, I started to cry. Little did I know that the next time that seat would be won would be fifteen years later, and it would be won by me.

It was quite an induction into politics and I've never been out of it since. In May 1958, the council elections were coming up again. We didn't seem to have much of a chance because the Unionists had a majority on the register. I borrowed fifty quid and I managed to split the vote. I won by twenty-seven votes and that was me a councillor!

Those three years, between 1958 and 1961, were the most important years in my political life. I didn't get paid for being a councillor. I had no money and I was rearing a small family. But I was absolutely obsessed with being in politics and being able to help people. I read all the National Insurance Acts and used to go down to the local tribunals representing people. I became known as the Perry Mason of the local tribunals!

When I was elected, I deliberately set out to prove that I wasn't a Catholic representative but that I was a non-sectarian representative. I remember Protestants coming to my door in 1958 and they would say 'Councillor Fitt, I'm a Protestant,' and I would say, 'Look, I don't care whether you're a Protestant or not.' Those people were living in exactly the same conditions as the Catholics and they were having the same problems. There was massive unemployment at the time and a whole lot of them were on the dole or on sickness benefit. I began to represent them and news of this travelled like wildfire all over the place. The more I helped them, the more they sent their relations to see me. It took a lot out of me. I had to neglect my own home and family, going to local tribunals and then going to meetings of the city council. I made a lot of friends in those three years.

In 1961, I defended the seat and I won it with a big, big majority. And then in 1962 the parliamentary seat came up for re-election. I went out and fought the seat and won. That gave me some sort of economic wherewithal to stay in politics. I had seven hundred quid a year and I thought I was a millionaire, but at least I was able to look after my wife and kids. In 1965, Terence O'Neill had taken over from Lord Brookeborough as Prime Minister and he called an election for November. I was very, very apprehensive about this election, because the history of Dock up until then had been that no political party had held the seat at successive elections. Here I was, the second time around, fighting against history, but I fought like hell and I won with an even bigger majority. So I beat the record in 1965.

In 1968, the civil rights movement began and I played a reasonably prominent part in that. I was interested in bringing in legislation which would help the underdog living in the Catholic ghettos in Northern Ireland. I went to Derry in October for the famous civil rights march. I had taken the precaution of bringing Labour MPs over, because I knew what was going to happen. I knew they were going to beat the hell out of us, and so I got some photographers over as well. I was grabbed by the police and they beat me over the head with a baton. The blood ran down my face and the cameras were there to see. It caused a great big furore. When I returned to Westminster, I made speech after speech saying, 'I got this for asking for the same rights for my constituents as you have for yours.'

The civil rights movement was totally justified, but it scared the life out of the Protestants, because they saw it as an attack on their privileges, which it actually wasn't. And that began the trouble. The Unionist underdog began to rebel against what he saw as concessions being given. There was awful fear in West Belfast. The Catholics thought that they were going to get slaughtered in their beds. I telephoned Jim Callaghan who was the then Home Secretary and pleaded with him to send the army in, because there was a real fear that a pogrom could have broken out in Northern Ireland. I remember what Jim Callaghan said to me. 'Gerry,' he said, 'I can get the army in, but it's going to be a devil of a job getting it out.' And how right he was proved to be.

I had a very nasty election in West Belfast, because the IRA were coming to the fore and they were beginning to attack me as being pro-Brit and so on. I won that election again in 1970. Then, in 1971, the IRA started shooting. When this happened it changed my whole political life, because I could never understand how the IRA could be guilty of some of the terrible atrocities that they committed. Internment came in August 1971 and that just tore the whole community asunder; the Catholic population were totally opposed to it.

In 1969, John Hume, Ivan Cooper, Paddy O'Hanlon and Paddy Devlin had been elected because of the civil rights agitation that was then taking place. There was great pressure on them to form a new political party. I had reservations about it, because I was from Belfast. I knew Belfast, I knew Protestants, but the others who were elected didn't have that same sort of political experience. They were Catholic representatives, as such. I formed, with the rest of them, the SDLP, the Social Democratic and Labour Party.

Bloody Sunday, in 1972, was a big watershed in politics in Northern Ireland. Because of that and our agitation, Stormont was abolished and then we came under direct rule. In 1973, we went to Sunningdale and we had the Sunningdale Conference. I thought then and I think now, and I will continue to think, that Sunningdale was by far the most hopeful development that we ever had politically in Northern Ireland since its creation. There were two tangents to it. One was the setting up of a Northern Ireland Executive, composed of both Catholics and Protestants. I thought that was a tremendous advance. In that executive, I was the deputy Prime Minister, the deputy chief executive. John Hume was the Minister for Commerce; Austin Currie was the Minister for Development; Paddy Devlin was the Minister for Health and Social Services; Ivan Cooper was the Minister for Community Relations. They were four of the most important offices in any government.

The second part of the Sunningdale Agreement was the part which actually killed Sunningdale. A provision was made for a Council of Ireland, which would involve the ministers in the Republic sitting with us. And that scared the living daylights out of the Unionists. When the executive fell in May of 1974, it caused great bitterness. People then realised that we should have done more to hold on to it.

The IRA were trying to kill me and they broke into my house in 1976. I will never forget the job I had getting them out. I had a licensed weapon at the time and, had I not had that, they would have beaten the hell out of me with iron bars. I felt particularly incensed, because I was a Catholic and these people were doing things allegedly in my name and in the name of Ireland. Whenever I appeared on television, I would make my position clear – that I detested them and everything that they stood for. I charged them with dragging the name of Ireland through the gutter and said they were not speaking on behalf of the Irish people.

But there were some of my colleagues in the SDLP who, when the IRA committed some terrible atrocity, would keep their heads down. It got to such a stage in 1979 that I left the party, because I felt I was on my own. In 1981, the hunger strike took place and that was a really big disaster for Northern Ireland. It tore the heart and soul out of the Catholic community and the Unionist community. The Unionists saw those hunger strikers as people who had murdered their friends, the

Catholics saw them as patriots or just some misguided young Irishmen, and it just tore them all apart.

I had an awful time during that period around my home on the Antrim Road. They used to gather around my home every night and throw stones and petrol bombs. They would stand outside the door and shout 'Gerry Fitt is a Brit.' It was the worst word they could have thrown. I was no more a Brit than I had ever been. I didn't go into politics as a Catholic or a Protestant, or as a Republican or Unionist. I went in as a working-class candidate to try to help people, but the whole thing was going awry.

In 1983, I had to defend my West Belfast seat. The SDLP was under the leadership of John Hume. Gerry Adams, the Sinn Féin candidate, came into the field and the SDLP deliberately put up a candidate. Again, it was a nasty election. I couldn't send out my election addresses, because the IRA wouldn't let the postman deliver them. Gerry Adams got 16,000 votes, Joe Hendron, who was the SDLP candidate, got 10,900 votes, and I got 10,400. The SDLP got that result with a pretty good election machine. I had no election machine at all. I only fought that election to prove to myself that I had done no wrong. Nobody ever said that I was a bad MP or a bad candidate or that I didn't represent them. Even in defeat, half of my votes had still come from across the political and religious divide.

All through this campaign my wife had asthma and she suffered very, very badly. How, in the name of God, she stood by me through all the terrible times with this asthma I do not know. We went over to England where I had just got a wee flat. Three weeks after the election, the police telephoned me to tell me my house was on fire. I flew back to Belfast but I wouldn't let my wife come with me, because she was very houseproud and I didn't want her to see the house in ruins. I went in and I saw how the house had been gutted and the windows broken and all the furniture had been taken out and burned in a bonfire. Just before I left the house, I looked down and saw on the ground what looked like confetti. I picked it up and I can feel that sickening feeling now. I don't think it will ever go away. It was my wedding photographs.

GARRET FITZGERALD

Garret FitzGerald (1926–2011) was born in Dublin,
the son of Desmond FitzGerald, Minister
for External Affairs and Defence in the Free
State Government. Following graduation from
University College Dublin, he was called to the
Bar but opted to join Aer Lingus. His parents
had always impressed the notion of public
service on him and, following another career as
a university lecturer, he joined Seanad Éireann
(the Irish Senate) in 1965. Thus began a long and
distinguished career in Irish politics. He entered
Dáil Éireann in 1969, became Minister for Foreign
Affairs in 1973, leader of Fine Gael in 1977, and
Taoiseach twice: 1981–2 and 1982–7. *All in a
Life. Garret FitzGerald: An Autobiography* was
published in 1992. This extract is taken from his
1991 *My Education* interview.

From Planes to Politics

My father wanted me to be a barrister – I think he had a feeling that it would be a respectable career. It would have been years before I could have got married if I had gone to the Bar but also I was interested in air transport. However, he couldn't accept that. When I took the job in Aer Lingus, he was very upset and didn't speak to me for several months. Then he saw that I was genuinely interested, and he relaxed, and our relationship was restored – happily, because he died only a month later.

In Aer Lingus, my interest lay in the economic operation of the airline – in routes, services, timetables, choice of aircraft, how to make the thing pay, how to make it efficient – and by the time I was twenty-six, I was in charge of the economic planning of the airline, which was a great opportunity for me. In order to take the decisions as to when to operate a flight or when not to, when it would pay or when it wouldn't, on what basis to open a new route, whether an aircraft would be economical or not, what was the optimum fare that would yield the maximum return, you had to have some criteria. I had to work out for myself the theoretical basis for answering these questions. I developed both a marginal costing structure and price economics theory in order to provide myself with the basis for making such decisions, and I didn't even know that this was economics.

Thus I came to economics in a curious way, having to invent it for myself in order to do my job and also by writing articles. I was journalistically inclined, as was my father. I eventually wrote for *The Irish Times* and they pushed me into writing about national economic matters, so I became an economist by popular acclaim, like saints in the old days before canonisation was introduced! I went back to UCD [University College Dublin] as a full-time lecturer in 1959, which was just thirteen years after I had left the college. I had been a part-time lecturer there for the previous three years.

On leaving Aer Lingus, I had gone into academic life and had become a consultant. I had in mind that the work I would be doing – particularly in relation to Irish industry preparing for free trade – would be a very good learning process to prepare myself for politics. Politics wasn't a firm decision, but it was certainly a possible path and then, in 1964, I finally took the decision to go into politics.

Politics has been a great educator for me, both in terms of domestic politics and experience in international affairs, and, indeed, in dealing with Northern Ireland, to which I suppose I brought a great deal of my background.

The basic issues of principle that I learned early on have remained with me and the concept of service – and of politics as one of the highest vocations of service – is something I learned very early on indeed in my life. On domestic affairs, my views have changed over time; I was very conservative when I was young, as my father had been in his views, but later in life I moved to being more of a social democrat and liberal.

A large part of my change of view was due to the influence of my own children – who are great educators of their parents – reinforced by the fact that I was teaching in UCD, where the students also challenged whatever implicit views I had during the many debates we had over coffee and in other places apart from the classroom. I found that my instinctive and inherited conservatism on many issues did not stand up to the challenge posed by the younger generation in the 1960s. I was forced to re-evaluate my position throughout that period, eventually establishing a different social and political stance to what I had had at the beginning. That is education in reverse – while you educate people, they are educating you.

For the last ten years, I have become interested in an aspect of knowledge that I have no capacity to cope with – the origins of the universe and the way the universe has developed, and also quantum physics. I have read a lot on these subjects but I can only grasp little bits here and there. These are two very important areas and it is a great pity that the educational system does not deal with them.

I think it is a mistake to divide education into the humanities and the sciences. I think these basic scientific issues are part of the humanities and children should not grow up without being exposed to the issues that are raised by the development of the universe from a certain point in time, say fifteen billion years ago, and about the nature of reality, which, when we look at it at the level of particles, is quite different from what we conceive it to be. I worry now that education is too narrow as it deprives people of any knowledge of these issues. I particularly regret that I didn't apply myself more to mathematics at school. I don't think I could ever have really grasped it, but I would have liked to have been able to understand more than I can now of these crucial matters.

My parents were largely the shapers of my life. They were remarkable people, very different, but deeply attached to each other. It was a very close marriage and both had very high standards. In fact, Joan once remarked that I am really half Presbyterian and half Jansenist! For me, the idea of public service was instinctive, coming from that background. It seemed to me from early on that one's task in life was to find ways of serving the community through whatever talents one had. My parents had sacrificed themselves so much in the period of the national movement. My father had been in gaol four times, which he had accepted quite readily, so that whole background of work in the national movement was obviously a profound influence.

FRANK M. FLANAGAN

Mayo-born Frank Flanagan (1946–2021) was a lecturer in education at Mary Immaculate College in Limerick for many years, and a regular contributor to *The Open Mind*. In 1993, I asked him to choose ten people who have made important contributions to educational thought over the past two thousand years and this became the genesis for the radio series *The Great Educators* in 1994. Frank came up with an interesting and varied list that included Socrates, Jesus Christ, Friedrich Fröbel, Jean-Jacques Rousseau, John Dewey and A.S. Neill. We later collaborated on a second series in 1999. From the first series, I have chosen an edited version of Frank's assessment of John Dewey. This was a different style of programme, with a prepared script by Frank and quotes from Dewey read by an actor.

Liberating The Child

John Dewey, who was to become one of the most powerful influences on educational thought in the twentieth century, was born in the town of Burlington, Vermont, in 1859. His father was proprietor of the local general store where, apparently, locals would foregather from time to time to discuss, with equal interest, affairs of both state and locality. According to one apocryphal story, the store window carried the legend: 'Hams and cigars: smoked and unsmoked'. The intimate small-town ethos of nineteenth-century Burlington played a large part in forming Dewey's educational outlook in two ways: one negative, one positive. On the negative side, he was convinced at a very early stage that the traditional, formal, desk-bound approach to schooling which was typified by the small town and rural schools of his childhood was futile. This kind of schooling was inadequate for the growing USA: a new society being born out of a simple agricultural economy which was being transformed by unprecedented industrialisation, immigration, rapid population growth, and drastic social change.

> [The old education] was predominantly static in subject matter, authoritarian in methods, and mainly passive and receptive from the side of the

young … the imagination of educators did not go beyond provision of a fixed and rigid environment of subject matter, one drawn moreover from sources altogether too remote from the experience of the pupil.

On the positive side, Dewey was convinced that the ordinary contacts of day-to-day community life, be they social, economic, cultural or political, provided real and significant learning situations. For Dewey, politics was not just a matter of national importance removed from the concern of the ordinary citizen but a matter of vital and immediate interest to the community. He believed that the school should prepare the child for active participation in the life of the community: he believed that education must break down, rather than reinforce, the gap between the experience of schooling and the needs of a truly participatory democracy.

Dewey graduated from the University of Vermont in 1879. After a period spent teaching high school, he went to Johns Hopkins University, where he gained his PhD degree in 1884. By his middle thirties he was head of the Department of Philosophy, Psychology and Pedagogy at the University of Chicago. It was here, in 1896, that Dewey established his famous 'Laboratory School'.

Dewey's Laboratory School was not intended to implement a structured pedagogical plan. It was intended as a laboratory in two senses: firstly, it was intended to facilitate research and experimentation into new principles and methods and, secondly, it was designed to allow the children to take an experimental approach to their own learning.

The furniture of the traditional school tells the story of traditional education; it is a story of submission, immobility, passivity and dependency.

> Just as the biologist can take a bone or two and reconstruct the whole animal, so, if we put before the mind's eye the ordinary school room, with its rows of ugly desks placed in geometrical order, crowded together so that there shall be as little moving room as possible, desks almost all of the same size, with just space enough to hold books, pencils and paper, and add a table, some chairs, the bare walls, and possibly a few pictures, we can reconstruct the only educational activity that can possibly go on in such a place. It is made for listening – because simply studying lessons out of a book is only another kind of listening; it marks the dependency of one mind upon

another ... it means, comparatively speaking, passivity ...

Dewey's approach was not a matter of whim or of arbitrary convictions about school design but a central feature of his philosophy. He wanted the Laboratory School to provide learners with the opportunity to create their own experience: to experiment, to enquire, to create. He wanted a classroom where children could move about, form groups, plan and execute activities; in short, learn for themselves under the direction and guidance of the teacher.

In Dewey's pedagogy, the teacher has two main functions. The teacher must guide the young through the complexities of life and give them opportunities to learn in the natural way, that is, by solving relevant problems. The teacher must also enable the young to cope adequately with contemporary conditions and to cope with the new tasks which an unpredictable future will bring.

The old model of education placed a premium on assignments, on private, isolated study, and on recitation. The mission of the Laboratory School was to find more effective ways of learning and teaching, to find ways of breaking down barriers between schools and their local communities and to find subject matter which would break the hold of traditional rote learning and symbol interpretation. This approach to schooling sets the pupils' experience at nought against the accumulated knowledge of the race: the pupil is made into a passive receptacle whose only function is to receive the structured subject matter which scholars have codified.

By contrast to the traditional approach, Dewey put the pupil at the centre of education as a wilful, purposive and active agent in the learning process:

> The child is the starting point, the centre, and the end. His development, his growth, is the ideal ... To the growth of the child all studies are subservient; they are instruments valued as they serve the needs of growth. Personality, character, is more than subject matter. Not knowledge or information, but self-realisation, is the goal. To possess all the world of knowledge and lose one's own self is as awful a fate in education as in religion.

The Laboratory School operated on three simple principles which informed Dewey's educational philosophy. The first principle was that the business of the school is to train children in co-operative and mutually helpful living – to help them to grow into community.

The second principle was that the foundation of all educative activity must be in the instinctive, impulsive activities of the child, and not in the presentation and application of structured, external material. This learning is rooted in the community. The individual and society cannot be considered in isolation one from the other.

Finally, the Laboratory School promoted the child's individual tendencies and activities. These were to be organised and directed to promote the idea of co-operative living. The learning process would take advantage of the child's individual tendencies and activities to reproduce, on the child's plane, the typical doings and occupations of the larger, mature society into which the child is finally to emerge.

In 1904, Dewey was appointed Professor of Philosophy at Columbia University and it was from this base that he articulated and spread the educational ideas which he had developed at the Chicago Laboratory Schools. They were to make him the most famous and influential educator of the twentieth century. He wrote, lectured and travelled extensively. On his retirement in 1930, he became Emeritus Professor at Columbia. It is one of the difficulties that Dewey presents to anyone who would present a short précis of his career that he lived to the age of ninety-three, active to the end – he married for the second time and started a second family at the age of eighty-seven.

A central concept in Dewey's philosophy of education, and to this day perhaps the most controversial, is his concept of growth. Dewey does not accept what are called 'teleological' explanations of human effort. These are explanations which place the significance of human effort in the distant future. They attempt to explain present events by future ones, such as the eventual dictatorship of the proletariat, the eventual attainment of the beatific vision, or whatever. In all cases they invoke some future perfection both to explain what we are doing now and to stipulate what we should be doing now. Teleological explanations are especially favoured by educational theorists: from a definition of some manner of idealised future, you can determine what we should be teaching our children in the present. Dewey rejects teleological explanations. He prefers an evolutionary account of human activity which freely acknowledges our ignorance of the future.

In Dewey's account, education is not a preparation for some idealised future. It is simply growth: the continuing reconstruction of our experience. It is not determined by any outside or independent aim or end. This is difficult for traditional educators to accept because they have always looked for the purpose and significance of education outside of the educational process itself. But the growth of which Dewey speaks is not growth towards some predetermined and externally imposed ideal or end.

There is no limit, in principle, to the possibilities of change, development and evolution – we simply do not know what the future holds. The child's relation to the curriculum is not the subordination of the child to the existing established knowledge, nor is it the abandonment of established existing knowledge for an anarchic, child-centred approach. Later, the child must come to learn the ways in which human knowledge has been structured into subjects or disciplines. But this is not the starting point – it is a development on the journey.

There must first be something in the child's experience which requires or demands this or that symbol, this or that discipline, this or that subject, before these mean anything to the child. The child's use of language, for instance, must spring from the child's own experience – whether this be actual or imaginative.

The child's education, the child's growth, is a gradual differentiation of this organic experience into what is represented by the traditional categories of knowledge such as geography, history, mathematics, literature, etc.

As well as growing up, the child grows out, into the world mediated by structured human knowledge.

Dewey's philosophy is about dealing with problems which arise out of real situations. It aims at control. It stresses that solutions to problems are tentative and to be judged by their usefulness. Its method is the method of science. It aims at the control of the environment and improvement of the environment by creative and reflective thought. The educational manifestation of scientific method is the project method associated with Dewey and his close follower, William H. Kilpatrick.

The project method certainly does not mean the transcription of 'information' from encyclopaedias and other sources of second-hand information, accompanied by illustrations to be hung on the classroom wall to impress important visitors. The principal value of a project is the experience of doing it, not the end result. In more general terms, the practical importance of the result of thinking is subsidiary to the process of thinking.

The control and direction of inquiry is central in Dewey's theory of education. Knowledge begins in doing; it is active. It is in the course of putting ideas to the test of experience that growth occurs. Dewey requires that pupils be given wide opportunities for purposive inquiry. This is as experienced in the project method. The pupil learns only by thinking about problems and trying to solve them for himself. It is like the difference between studying a map and making a journey: while the map is a useful guide for the traveller, it is not a substitute for the experience of travelling.

Dewey is sometimes associated with the worst excesses of so-called 'progressive' education: a do-as-you-please approach – which, it must be said, exists more often in people's imaginations than in actual classrooms. He was, however, forced to distance himself on a number of occasions from those who claimed to be his disciples.

Dewey's contribution to the development of education in the twentieth century has been incalculable if not without its controversies. His greatest contribution has been to liberate the education of children from the dead hand of tradition and from what he himself has called the 'static cold-storage ideal of knowledge'. He forged a theory and practice of education which can be relevant to contemporary industrial and social progress without becoming the slave of either:

The school is primarily a social institution. Education being a social process, the school is simply that form of community life in which all those agencies are concentrated that will be most effective in bringing the child to share in the inherited resources of the race, and to use his own powers for social end. Education, therefore, is a process of living and not a preparation for future living.

CHARLES HANDY

Charles Handy was born in 1932 in Co. Kildare, the son of a Church of Ireland archdeacon. He became a teacher, social philosopher, broadcaster and writer. His many books exploring the big issues that face society include *The Future of Work*; *Understanding Organizations*; *The Empty Raincoat: Making Sense of the Future*; *The Elephant and the Flea: New Thinking for a New World*; and *Myself and Other More Important Matters* (a memoir). I first met him in the mid-1980s when I was preparing a radio series entitled *The Future of Work*, and his prophetic book of the same name became the core of the series. We became good friends and he was a regular contributor to my radio programmes over two decades. In 2019, he published *21 Letters on Life and Its Challenges* – letters written to his four grandchildren. The book is a wonderful overview of his ideas (there should be copies in every school!). His contribution here is taken from the series *My Education*. After a ten-year career with Shell plc, Charles joined the London Business School and went to the Massachusetts Institute of Technology to do a Master of Science in Management degree.

My Portfolio Life

On my second day there, I had a meeting which, again, changed my life. I met Warren Bennis, who was Professor of Organisational Behaviour, a title I'd never heard before. He was a young rising star of this new field of human behaviour and organisations and he had gathered in his house that evening all the stars of the field, who, twenty-five years later, are still great people. They persuaded me that what really mattered in organisations is not the money, or the market, or the machines, or the computers, but the *people*.

I had a fascinating year with Warren Bennis, who is now one of my greatest friends and lives in California. He was another of those key people in my life at a key point in time who helped shape my world. That was still a slightly artificial world and some of my old upbringing in the rectory was beginning to come back to me. I was realising that what I really wanted was to help people who were worse off than me. I found myself very uneasy, sitting working with rather elitist, spoilt young men and women who were going off to earn huge salaries.

After ten years there, my father died. I went to his funeral, back in Ireland, at the old church that he had served for forty years. The place was packed with people crying and saying, 'This man meant more to us than anything else.' I suddenly realised that he had lived a rather special life, and the things that I had run away from, even despised, were actually incredibly valuable. So, in a way, to apologise to him, I resigned my professorship, which was a crazy thing to do. It was a guaranteed job to sixty-five, a comfortable life and long vacations. I resigned all that and went to run a small centre, which happened to be based behind St George's Chapel in Windsor Castle, which educated the new bishops and the up-and-coming clergy who might become bishops. In between running these courses, I also held rather high-level meetings of about twenty-five leaders of society convened by Prince Philip, who was my boss, ultimately, to talk about social justice in society, the changing nature of work and the changing distribution of incomes, and such things. So there I was, on a clergy salary, living in a rectory, helping people less fortunate than myself. My life had gone full circle.

I met six thousand people in four years. I sat at the feet of a hundred and ten theologians over that period. It was an amazing learning experience for me. I was bombarded with the ideas of very interesting people and it broadened my horizons enormously. I had a five-year contract, but I always think that you should leave one year before it is expected. By this time, I was actually talking and writing about what I call 'the future of work' and basically saying that a lot of people would have to spend a lot of their lives living what I called a 'portfolio life' – by their wits, bits and pieces of work, self-employed if you like, with a range of clients and customers and a range of skills. And wouldn't it be a very good idea if I actually tried to do that!

People thought I was crazy. I was forty-nine by then and at the height of my career. People expected me to go off and head a business school or a university – and that would have been an ambitious thing to do. Instead, I resigned from everything and went back to my flat in Putney in south London and my cottage in East Anglia to write books and do a bit of teaching. I had a £5,000 contract with the London Business School to do occasional bits of teaching and that was going to be my sole income.

It was frightening,, actually, but also incredibly freeing because up until then, half of me was Charles Handy but half of me was professor of this or head of that. I had to look over my shoulder to make sure I was saying the right thing. Suddenly I was all Charles Handy. I could be myself. I could say what I liked. I could arrange my life totally differently.

For instance, my wife and I decided to work one hundred days a year on what you might call 'money-making things' – things that produce money – and one hundred days a year on study; that is, writing books and researching them. We would give fifty days a year to charitable causes; my tithing to society, as it were. That's two hundred and fifty days, which leaves one hundred and fifteen days for leisure, which is actually two days per weekend and a fortnight's holiday. By doing it this way, we could take two months off in the year and spend one month in Italy and one month in America if we wanted. It looked extravagant, but then, of course, we would have to work on Saturdays and Sundays, which we would use for study time, which meant reading and writing in our cottage in Norfolk.

It seemed to us to be an example of what I call 'liberated upside-down thinking' – the old tradition I learned from Oxford: question everything. Why work five days a week and have two days at weekends? Why not parcel it out in other ways?

Economically, after a little while, we survived. My wife did something very important. Hitherto, she had been the mother of my children and the company of my bedroom and my social life and so on. She had her own interests. She had been an interior designer and a marriage counsellor. We decided to become full partners at work and that she would be my managing partner – she would be my agent, my organiser, and she would arrange my work. That was an enormously useful discipline for me.

When you are working on your own, you can be besieged by people. Some of them could be interesting, but a lot of them might not be. Elizabeth took over all the fielding of all that – she organised my life. She raised money for advances for my books and she took on several lucrative contracts, speaking and teaching in organisations. We very soon found that we only needed to sell fifty days a year of my time to produce enough money. We also took a very crucial decision – that we didn't want to be as rich as possible, we just wanted to be rich enough.

Now that sounds very privileged but, if you think about it, most people really only sell fifty days of their time to other people and they clutter up the rest of the year preparing for that. We disciplined ourselves: fifty days selling, fifty days for preparation and one hundred days of study.

In a sense, the place I ran away from is the place I have ended up in. Okay, it's a flat in Putney and a cottage in Norfolk, but it's all about trying to discover the truth and helping other people to do that too; it's about preaching a little, which I tend to do now on the radio; teaching a little, which I do now through books more than anything else; helping people who are less fortunate to learn about themselves: and to live out that truth. It's a little rectory in Kildare. I can't escape those first seven years.

SEAMUS HEANEY

I was privileged to enjoy a working relationship with the man from Bellaghy (1939–2013). He was more than generous with his time, on which there were unrelenting demands, and he was a regular contributor to interviews, features and documentaries. When he won the 1995 Nobel Prize for Literature, I joined in the national elation and celebration. How could I best pay tribute to him for this wonderful achievement? I remembered a talk I had recorded in 1982: the poet's opening address to the World Congress of the International Reading Association, held in Dublin. The address, entitled 'Words Alone?', was given to a packed audience in the National Concert Hall. For some reason I had never broadcast it, but maybe now was its time since the debasement of language in the modern world was the sole theme of his address. This excerpt shows how his words are even more relevant four decades later.

On The Debasement of Language

'Words, words, words' [*Hamlet*, Act 2, Scene 2]. Hamlet's famous retort to Polonius, its impatience and irony, its modern distrust, its nostalgia for authentic speech, is one of the commonest and most succinct reminders of how the debasement of language is a debasement of experience and a trivialising of the things of the world. And the retort came, it is well to remember, in answer to the question 'What do you read, my lord?' Already for Hamlet, the first of alienated men, the one for whom the world had lost its savour, books were a potentially disabling force. Instead of enhancing the savour of experience and keeping it fresh in the holds of print, the written page was neutralising the essential tang of experience, robbing it of its individual flavour and weight. And if that feeling was possible for the prince of Denmark in the opening decade of the seventeenth century, how much more universally possible it has become for us in the last decades of the twentieth century – in the world of super propaganda, corporate money, political rhetoric, economic mystification, universal jargon, universal publicity and international 'communicator-ese'. The world has become so voluble and fast-talking that language itself is suspect – so many duplicitous communiques and statements and reports, so many appeasing half-truths and glossy half-lies, so many images sold, people and products promoted, so many lives taken or broken in the cause of implacable slogans that the conscious and scrupulous intelligence can only regard the world at best as a jabbering marketplace dealing in a fake currency and at worst a monstrous welter of self-interest and exploitation. And because of the apparent impossibility of uttering a fully personal voice into the general swill of communication, we may accede to the vapid verbal universe that we are doomed to inhabit, and sink imperceptibly into our personal limbo-land with all our old responsible grain-worn language attachments hermetically silenced. We may become like Eliot's 'hollow men'.

MICHAEL D. HIGGINS

Michael D. Higgins (*b.* 1941) is a poet, philosopher and former lecturer in political science and sociology in the University of Galway. He was a Labour TD for Galway West and was Minister for Arts, Culture and the Gaeltacht from 1992 to 1997. He is currently more than halfway through his second term as president of Ireland. In this extract from the 1992 Open Mind Guest Lecture on the theme 'Education for Freedom', he appeals for 'a pedagogy of love'.

A Pedagogy of Love

At this moment, we are facing the choice of a new relationship to the planet and each other. We can educate for regression to brutal self-interest or we can educate for peace and true security, for openness. What is required now is a critical capacity developed within an educational system where creativity is made central.

We should not despair. We should remember Bertrand Russell:

> Meantime, the world in which we exist has other aims. But it will pass away, burned up in the fire of its own hot passions; and from its ashes will spring a new and younger world, full of fresh hope, with the light of morning in its eyes.

If we engage the connections between science, technology and society, it is possible for us, even yet, to become a symbol-using, rather than a symbol-abusing, species, and to experience the joy of our humanness, made immanent.

It is possible for us, as Raymond Williams put it, to be the arrow not the target, within the technology of television and culture.

Let us choose then the pedagogy of love. Let us allow the pedagogy of fear to fall away from our institutions, our practice and our personalities.

Let us make education a right, accessible through one's entire life.

Let us have real democracy, elective and accountable, not only in a geographical sense, but in a community sense. Let us elect our representatives for educational accountability from within the sectors involved and from outside. Why should we settle for less, unless we are conceding democracy itself?

The new dawn of which Russell wrote will only be possible if we refuse to surrender education to the passing fad of neo-utilitarianism.

In the next century, we will be asked to be many things but, above all, we will be most useful to the human family and ourselves if we are holistic.

I am mindful of the issue of resources for education. I have supported and will support the political fight for adequate resources and their direction, in particular, to areas of disadvantage. But we do not have to choose between activity on that issue and related issues, such as in-service training and renewal, and we can no longer neglect the debate about the very nature of education itself.

In conclusion, then, may I say that there is too much that is covert in Irish education. There is far too much piecemeal decision-making. The antipathy to intellectual ideas, to philosophy and theory in education, and in the social sciences in general, must be ended.

For example, so many within teaching, so many parents, would welcome a debate on education's place in a New World Communicative Order.

They would welcome, too, the tension between the control functions of education and its responsibilities for enhancing and releasing creativity, being set in tension and such tension being critically examined.

It is a time for courage, a time to demand and ensure that, in our country, education will never again be allowed to destroy the wonderment of a child. Rather that, heroically, we will begin to make our way back to that wonderment and live in peace with each other and our planet.

SHIRLEY HUGHES

Shirley Hughes (1927–2022) was born in the Wirral Peninsula on the outskirts of Liverpool. As a writer and illustrator for children, she won worldwide fame and popularity. This contribution is based on an interview I did with her in her home in Notting Hill, London, in 2007, to mark her eightieth birthday, which was broadcast on RTÉ Lyric FM in 2008. Shirley was a voracious reader as a child and the books she read then greatly influenced her choice of career. As she said in another interview, 'There will always be story and there will always be the need for story.'

Words and Pictures

I always saw pictures and stories as strongly interwoven. Thomas Henry's wonderful line drawings for Richmal Crompton's *William* books made me want to be an illustrator. My whole career has been influenced by people like Ernest Shepard whose masterful illustrations for *The Wind in the Willows* made the characters and the background come to life. I always wanted to be like him. Then there was Edward Ardizzone, whom I knew. When you looked at a page of his work, the magic of the line opened you to a third dimension. I really loved Will Heath Robinson. He belonged to the era of the illustrated classics. He had the good fortune and the bad luck to be famous for those wild inventions, but as an illustrator he had a macabre side. His illustration of *A Midsummer Night's Dream* was absolutely brilliant.

The young Shirley's mind was set. Illustration would be her career. She went to West Kirby High School where art was 'O.K. We did nice pictures once a week under the tutelage of the highly-strung, skeletal Miss Griffiths … but most of the artwork I did was done at home.' She moved on to Liverpool Art School for a fashion drawing course, where she learned how to cut material and design costumes – experience which would stand to her later as an illustrator. That course lasted only a year and – anxious to move away from The Wirral – Shirley persuaded her mother to let her go to Oxford. She duly enrolled at Ruskin College where she turned up in 'a cashmere jumper and pearls when everyone else was in paint-bespattered overalls – so I had to change very quickly!'

Ruskin was mainly a fine art college but there was a very good lithography teacher there who encouraged her to do illustration. 'By this time I had spent a summer as a general dogsbody with a repertory company and – wonderful though it was – I knew then that I would never have the commitment for acting, so now it was *definitely* illustration for me. After all, a book is a kind of theatre in itself, isn't it?' Oxford was a bit overwhelming initially – there were all sorts of cliques and 'sets' – but Shirley overcame that and made her own friends.

One of the great highlights of Oxford was Kenneth Clark's lectures on the history of art.

I knew nothing about art history but he opened doors for me. From the very first lecture when he showed a slide of the Rembrandt etching *Christ Shown to the People*, the hairs stood up on the back of my neck. Door after door opened for me. The following year I went to Florence to see the real thing and I've never stopped looking at paintings since.

After Oxford, getting started on a career was difficult. Line drawing for children's fiction was a wonderful apprenticeship but very badly paid and it was only when the author Noel Streatfeild saw Shirley's work and asked her to illustrate her fiction that the major breakthrough came. In the meantime, she took on everything including school texts (*See Tom run. Run, Tom, run!* doesn't give one much scope!) but eventually things improved – particularly when Shirley worked with Dorothy Edwards (of *My Naughty Little Sister* fame). They became friends and soulmates and went on publicity tours together. 'Dorothy was a brilliant storyteller. She would have her audience enthralled, while I stood at the back and did drawings! We were the Laurel and Hardy of the book circuit.'

Romance entered Shirley's life in the most unlikely circumstances. She was visiting a friend who had a small baby. The drain outside her basement flat was blocked and all sorts of muck was swirling about. The baby was crying. She couldn't unblock the drain and was in despair. Along came John – the tenant in the upper flat – who rolled up the sleeve of his immaculate white shirt and plunged his arm into the drain. 'The muck all went away. The baby stopped crying. The sun came out and I thought, *this man knows what he's doing.*' John asked

Shirley out and they had a long and happy marriage until, sadly, he died in 2007.

John was an architect so they had an empathy for each other's work. They would go regularly to Florence and he became a very good painter and etcher in later life. John was a great support in the early days when Shirley was juggling a freelance career with motherhood – they eventually had three children. They moved into Notting Hill in 1954 – a very different Notting Hill. 'It was a very run-down, tough area, houses with multiple occupancy, race riots and so on, but gradually it changed. I'm very glad we moved here, and I'm still here, over fifty years later.' Notting Hill became the backdrop for Shirley's first picture book – *Lucy and Tom's Day*, and for many of her subsequent books.

I was always drawn to realism, portraying the child's real world. I observed children very carefully. I always kept sketchbooks [her autobiography – *A Life Drawing* – teems with sketches from her long career] and once you draw something you never forget it. I'm always being asked are the children in my books my own children or actual Notting Hill children. They're not anybody's children! It's that experience of observation that enables me to draw children – the way they stand and move, their whole body language. The pictures and the words unfold in my head, and once I've got the words right I make a 'rough' and the essence of the book is in that 'rough'. I work with energy and freedom when I'm doing that and the great test of professionalism is to get that same freedom into the finished drawing.

Success came to Shirley with her stories based on the little daily dramas she observed about her. *Dogger* (1977) is the classic story of the much-loved soft toy which goes missing (I remind Shirley that if I read that story once to my five-year-old son, I must have read it five hundred and ninety times ...). *Alfie Gets in First* (1981) tells of the boy who locks his mother out of the house. With success came awards (*Dogger* won the prestigious Kate Greenaway Medal), literary festivals, school tours and children's (very honest) letters, but none of these interrupted Shirley's prolific output of both writing/illustrating her own books and illustrating other authors' work. The output now runs into the hundreds. Shirley acknowledges the importance of a good editor. She speaks warmly of the legendary Kaye

Webb, who founded Puffin Books, and of Judy Taylor, Ann McNeil and Margaret Clarke of The Bodley Head. She acknowledges also the importance of the advent of Walker Books in 1980 – the brainchild of the 'single-minded' Sebastian Walker.

Her four score years have not dimmed Shirley Hughes's passion for her work and for the world of children one whit. She is concerned that today's children are over-stimulated visually by a succession of electronic images coming at them relentlessly. 'There is a need to slow the pace down. Young children need the opportunity to explore at their own pace – and still images are very important here. Pause, turn the page, turn back, animate the story for themselves.' And she remains convinced that – as she told me twenty-five years ago – 'there will always be story and there will always be the need for story'. She recalls visiting Belfast at the height of the Troubles, watching a 'wonderful librarian' telling the story of the three Billygoats Gruff to a group of little ones in the courtyard of a block of flats.

They were spellbound until a posse of military came through. The older children threw missiles at the soldiers and the little ones followed the older children. When it was all over and the older ones disappeared into the flats, the little ones came back to the librarian and implored her to go on with the story. I was astonished. It just illustrated the power of story.

JOHN HUME

A civil rights activist in Northern Ireland, John Hume (1937–2020) was elected a Member of Parliament in 1969. He was a co-founder and leader of the Social Democratic and Labour Party. He was later a member of the European Parliament and one of the principal architects of the Peace Process in Northern Ireland. In 1998, he was jointly awarded (with David Trimble) the Nobel Prize for Peace. He gave the Open Mind Guest Lecture in 1994 under the theme 'Leaving the Past Behind'. In this extract, he makes an appeal to harness the Irish diaspora across the world.

Harnessing the Diaspora

Difference is of the essence of humanity. Difference enriches humanity, and diversity enriches humanity. The peoples of Europe decided to respect their differences and to recognise that the divisions of centuries couldn't be healed in a week or a fortnight. They built institutions which respected their differences, which permitted them to work their common ground together, which is economics – bread on your table and a roof over your head; the right to existence, which is the most fundamental right, plus the right to a decent life. By spilling their sweat, and not their blood, in building together, they broke down the barriers of centuries. The new Europe is gradually evolving, and it will continue to evolve.

I believe that that is what we have to do on this small island: respect our differences, build institutions which respect those differences, but which create the framework within which our healing process can take place, and within which we too can then work our very substantial common ground, which is economic. The first step on the road has been taken – a total cessation of violence – and it wasn't easy to get there. The decisions of the paramilitary organisations – who themselves are a product of our history – to lay down their arms will, I hope, prove to be historic decisions. The fact that we meet for the first time in a long time, in a peaceful atmosphere, should help us face up to that major challenge, because you do not heal the divisions of centuries, or the distrusts and prejudices of centuries, in a week or a fortnight. It is no longer the 1920s. When those military checkpoints leave our border, there will, in effect, be no border on this island. We are all part of a single market of Europe, with its free movement of goods, people and services. Once we start interacting together on the island for the first time in economic terms, some independent people have already forecasted that developing the trade among our island people could create up to 75,000 jobs. But the real border remains.

The real border is in the hearts and minds of our people. There are those who would tell us that partition is the problem of this country; it is not. What partition did was to institutionalise the real problem, which was already there and had been there for centuries. If Wolfe Tone wanted to unite the Irish people in 1798, they must have been divided. That division has been there for centuries. Partition simply institutionalised it and made it worse. The removal of the economic border leaves the real border in the hearts and minds of our people, and that's the challenge that we have to face up to in this new European world. We are living today in a post-nationalist world. There are those around Europe who still think that the nation state is something that is eternal. The nation state is only an era in history.

Once upon a time, there were city states. Once upon a time, we had high kings and we had kings, and then we had clan chieftains. The nation state has only been an evolutionary period in history, and when the history of the world is written, it will have proved to be one of the worst periods because it caused not only imperialism but two world wars.

Today's world is a much smaller world than in the 1920s, when the parents and grandparents of people in this room and people listening to me would hardly have left their own district in their lives. Today, you can sit in your own room and watch what's happening right across the world as it happens. There's no such thing as an independent country left in this world. We are interdependent. We cannot live apart. We are living in a post-nationalist world. The old traditional attitudes shouldn't harden our attitudes when we come to a table. We should recognise that the legacy of our past is still there; the divided people. But let us also work our common ground together, which is noncontroversial, and again I'm talking about economics.

We in this small island are the biggest wandering people in the world. In the last census in the United States of America, forty-two million people signed that they were of Irish extraction, from both our traditions.

Most of their ancestry were driven from this island by famine, by injustice, by intolerance. Yet in today's world, they have come to the top – in politics, in government, in economics; in all fields. We have had presidents of the United States of Irish extraction, prime ministers of Canada, Australia and New Zealand of Irish extraction, and likewise leaders of the business communities in all those countries. The time has come to harness that and to define Irishness today, not just simply those who live on the island, but let us harness the Irish diaspora as we tackle our economic problems, to use their influence across the world to market the products of our small industries on this island, and to seek the inward investment that will provide the basic right of existence to all our people. And doing that together, in both our traditions, using our links with both our traditions across the world, spilling our sweat and not our blood, will make a major contribution to the healing process and to the breaking down of barriers between our people.

BRENDAN KENNELLY

Brendan Kennelly (1936–2021) was born in the village of Ballylongford, Co. Kerry, where his father owned a public house. He was educated locally and was fortunate to come under the influence of an inspirational teacher, Jane Agnes McKenna. He came to Dublin to work for the Electricity Supply Board but soon discovered that writing and the study of the English language were his real vocations in life. He pursued that study in Trinity College Dublin, went on to lecture there and eventually became Professor of Modern Literature. A very prolific and popular poet, he was a regular contributor to radio and television programmes. His many volumes of poetry include *The Book of Judas*; *A Kind of Trust*; *Cromwell*; *Islandman*; and *A Time for Voices: Selected Poems 1960–1990*. His reflection here on the Kerry childhood that shaped him, as man and poet, is adapted from his 1993 *My Education* radio interview.

Made in Kerry

The village of Ballylongford is in the form of a cross. There is a lovely old church at the left arm of the cross and out beyond the head of the cross there is Lislaughtin Abbey, about which there are tremendous stories. Father Ferris, another great old priest who used to translate Dante into Irish and get us to memorise history, used to send us out every April the sixth to clean all the graves of the parish, because, in his view, that was the day that Lislaughtin was destroyed by Cromwellian soldiers. Further down is Carrigafoyle Castle, which was occupied by the O'Connors, and behind that there is a wonderful island called Carraig Island. About twenty years ago I went through a depression and I remember thinking – what is my life about, at all? Into my mind came a man out of that island. He started to tell me things and I wrote them down. I wrote the poem, *The Island Man*, and worked hard at it for a year or so and I suddenly realised that he was helping me to express myself. Father Ferris, a wonderful man who used to say a Mass for Jesse James, was born on the other side of the parish, in Asdee. Old men like Father Ferris come back into your mind and they help you understand yourself. That to me is learning – the inexplicable, irrational influences of the dead on your living character. I don't fully understand it, but why should I need to when it makes me happy?

Old people chuckle out of their own wisdom and perhaps even out of their bitterness and scepticism and they say things to a child in such a way that the child's interest is stimulated. It was a great experience for me in the late '40s when I was still at school to come home and go into the pub and draw pints for the fellows. That was my introduction to the curious freedom in conversation that marks a good pub. I think it was Yeats's father who said that every Irishman should talk as if he had just taken two large glasses of whiskey. After a few pints, men tell stories and release themselves and that to me has always been the peculiar delight of a public house. After thirty-five years, I still think of the men I met there and their names come into my mind and the way they sang their songs and told their stories. They were very kind fellows as well. It was a very poor time and they didn't have much money, but they really appreciated the drink and each other's company. There were a few of them that used to sing songs and they come back to my mind like ghosts, only they are like living ghosts.

Richard Broderick celebrates
This winter's first and only fall of snow
With a midnight rendering
Of *The Bonny Bunch of Roses O*

And Paddy Dineen is rising
With *On Top of the Old Stone Wall*
His closed eyes respect the song.
His mind's a festival.

And now *Ramona* lights the lips
Of swaying Davy Shea
In a world of possibilities
This is the only way.

His face a summer morning
When the sun decides to smile
Tom Keane touches enchantment
With *Charming Carrig Isle.*

I've seen men in their innocence
Untroubled by right and wrong.
I close my eyes and see them
Becoming song.

All the songs are living ghosts
And long for a living voice.
O may another fall of snow
Bid Broderick rejoice!

(from 'Living Ghosts')

The old should be treated with respect and should be loved and, above all, they should be listened to, because they have a lot to say and they say it with devilment! There is nothing as lovely as a smile on an old face and a bit of a twinkle in an old person's eye when he is telling you a lie, or when he is making up a story for you and you know he is telling you a lie. I remember Paddy Brandon saying to me one day, 'Take me home and wash my toes.' So I took him up to the little room where he was living and I took off the shoes and washed the toes. He began to say, 'It's very hard now to wash your toes when you are my age, but I could tell you stories about these toes,' and he started telling me these old yarns. That was wonderful and I never forgot it, whereas I have forgotten an awful lot of lectures about the ambiguity of philosophy!

I went to a second-level school in Tarbert, which was run by an amazing woman. Her name was Jane Agnes McKenna and she had two teachers, Pat and

Alice Carey. She taught languages and some kind of commerce, but her emphasis was on words and trying to tell the truth. She used to get very angry about telling lies and it was the only thing she would slap you for. Her love of literature was genuine and profound. She would get us all to say speeches from Shakespeare. It was great to hear the lads reciting *Macbeth*, *Hamlet* and *Othello* in north Kerry accents. The best way to experience words is to commit them to memory. As you walk along the street or sit down in pubs and talk to friends, you can allow your mind to be visited by words that you learned many years ago. Miss McKenna, as we used to call her, handed us this ability to be haunted, to leave our hearts and minds open to Shakespeare, to Latin, to French and to Irish. We had to write a lot at the weekend and then we would have to stand up in class and read it out, and read out other people's writing as well. It was a life of expression.

Later, when I suffered from moments of depression, I learned that expression is the best way to heal depression and that it is necessary at every level to utter yourself. Silence is a great act of expression. Miss McKenna taught us to be silent every evening. I have kept that habit, particularly in the morning when I wake up and my mind is full of dreams. I can sit there and write, without trying to explain and, above all, without trying to analyse the dreams that have visited me during the night.

ALICE LEAHY

Alice has spent her working life as a professional carer. Born in 1941, she qualified as a nurse in Dublin and worked with various voluntary groups that cared for people in the deprived areas of the city. Alice became particularly involved with the homeless and eventually set up, with others, the organisation TRUST (now the Alice Leahy Trust), which offers practical care and rehabilitation to people experiencing homelessness. She traces her own commitment to this issue back to the trust and confidence that was instilled in her during her own upbringing.

Building Trust

I grew up in Annsgift, just outside Fethard in County Tipperary. My father and mother were two great people and I suppose it is only now I realise how powerful and how marvellous they were. We were very close to the land and in fact five generations of my father's family lived on that land. They didn't own it, but they tilled the soil as if it was their own. We didn't feel bitterness because the land wasn't ours. My father loved every blade of grass and every animal on the land as if they were our own. I remember, as we walked through the fields, my father looking at the animals, encouraging me to respect nature and saying that one didn't have to own it to respect it, that we were all part of the world.

The land belonged to the Hughes family; Olivia Hughes was a driving force in the country markets, the ICA [Irish Countrywomen's Association] and the League of the Blind in the early days. They certainly had a great influence on my life. They owned the land and had what we would call a 'Big House' there, but we depended on one another. We were never made to feel they were superior and we were inferior. We treated one another with great respect and care. In fact, we looked forward to their visits when we were small. They would come and see us and bring us presents and tell us about the parts of the world they had come from. Through them, we were in touch with professional people like doctors, dentists and eye specialists – people who can often be seen as aloof, but who we saw as real people who were part of our lives.

I went to school through the fields – and there was nothing romantic about going to school through the fields. If you got wet, you were wet for the day. I liked the national school and I remember my own national school teacher with great affection. Julia Ryan was a woman from Kerry whose husband had died when she was young. I think the mixture of boys and girls was very healthy. We had to go to the well for our spring water for whatever we had at lunchtime and we had to collect *cipín*s [little sticks] from the ditches to light the fire.

Secondary school was something I just passed through. It was the first time I noticed any kind of class distinction in our society. We didn't play tennis and we didn't play music. Some of that could have been due to the fact that, geographically, we were so far out from the town, but money was also a factor. I didn't find any great challenge at secondary school, although credit is due to my teachers for helping me get through my exams.

A lot of my real education was taking place outside the school, anyway. Olivia Hughes played the cello with the opera society in Clonmel and she always took us to the opera – something a lot of people would have been excluded from, even in those times. There was also an amateur dramatic group in Fethard and my parents would take us to that. We were also involved in Macra na Tuaithe [now Foróige], and the Hughes family gave us part of their house to do up as a youth club. It was a very active youth club, where we had debates, question times and visiting speakers. We did weaving; we collected sheep's wool from the ditches and carded it and made long ropes. We knitted squares for the refugees. We also ran the youth club ourselves, with Olivia's help and encouragement, with a chairman, a secretary and a treasurer, and taking minutes at a very young age.

My father was a very resourceful man and, in many ways, was ahead of his time. He was into things like recycling before the word was even invented. Everything we had was used and re-used. A family near us used to give us a goose every year and the goose feathers were kept to make cushions and pillows. We embroidered old canvas bags to make the cushions; we used all the raw material we could get. We grew our own vegetables; we kept hens; we got milk from the Hughes family; we always had access to a good supply of fruit. We used tea leaves to sprinkle on the floors to keep the dust down; we collected all our firewood; we had to sew and iron and knit; we preserved eggs and made jams and chutneys; we used eggshells to keep the water in when we were painting and we were always encouraged to paint and draw and to make puzzles.

My mother had three old aunts: one lived to be one hundred and the others lived into their nineties. One of them was a nurse and we used to love visiting her. She had worked in Daisy Hill Hospital in Newry and I suppose she gave me an insight into nursing. We grew up caring for the elderly and visiting the old county home, so it was probably inevitable that I should become a nurse. I didn't want to go to England, so I wrote off to different hospitals in Ireland. One of the eye specialists at Baggot Street Hospital introduced me to the matron, and I got an interview and started in Baggot Street.

It was hard. We had to do a lot of the work that would now be done by domestic staff, as well as going to lectures and studying. When we were on the wards, we had to light the fires and clean the wheels of the beds. We had to be very resourceful. There was nothing disposable in those days, but there was nothing new in all of that for me.

I went on to work in the Rotunda and it was there that I got involved with Voluntary Service International [VSI], a voluntary group that was involved in very practical work in deprived areas of the city. There was an old complex of flats in the north inner city and there I made contact with VSI, which ran workshops with the mothers and children and the older people there. It was a most interesting time of my life in the city. I got very involved with VSI and the adoption society in the Rotunda and a lot of the mothers I met there I would meet again later outside in the community.

I was very taken with a quotation from the founder of VSI, which I suppose is now a part of my own philosophy – 'The world is a poem, an immense poem, which people have no time to read because they are busy in their offices.' That was written many years ago and I think it is still true today.

PATRICK LINDSAY

Patrick Lindsay (1914–1993) was born in Dublin but moved to Co. Mayo with his family at a very young age. He was educated at St Muredach's College, Ballina, Co. Mayo, and University College, Galway, where he pursued a master's degree in classics. A brief and unsettled career in teaching followed (he taught in seventeen schools in three and a half years!) before Patrick reached his real objective – Dublin and the study of law at University College Dublin and King's Inns. A master of oratory and a keen student of the English language, Patrick embarked on a glittering legal career, rising to the position of senior counsel and eventually to Master of the High Court. His other great interest was politics and he first stood for election at the age of twenty-two. He eventually made it to Dáil Éireann in 1954 as a Fine Gael deputy and became part of the coalition government. He became the country's first Minister for the Gaeltacht in 1956. His wit and classical background made him a formidable opponent, both in court and parliament, and he had many memorable jousts with his opponents, notably Donogh O'Malley. Patrick Lindsay published his memoir, *Memories*, in 1993. His contribution here is based on his interview for the series *My Education*.

Law and Politics

I got into law through a man who had tremendous influence on me. He had been a TD for north Mayo in the 1920s – the late Professor Michael Tierney, ultimately president of UCD [University College Dublin]. He and my father were great friends and my father wrote to him when I abandoned ship in Cavan Royal School and went to Dublin with nothing. Michael Tierney made me tutor and guardian to a very brilliant lad, now dead, called Eoin McWhite. He died in a motor accident while he was our ambassador to The Hague. Mahaffy of Trinity used to say that Oscar Wilde was the only guy who understood the middle voice in Greek, but I was fortunate to meet another, and that was Eoin McWhite. Teaching him helped to pay the rent on the flat and I did grinds as well. Then Michael Tierney asked me if I would edit book twelve of Virgil's *Aeneid* for Browne and Nolan's, for which I received what was, in the 1940s, a massive fee of one hundred guineas. I paid law fees, I paid outstanding digs money and everything else and I finished up on Saturday with nothing but dirty fingernails and coppers and memories. I would say I was a rake with a touch of class and making progress all the time.

The man on whom I modelled my own career was the late James FitzGerald-Kenney. His family were landed gentry from Belcarra, outside Castlebar. He was a member of the Dáil in 1927 and was appointed Minister for Justice after the O'Higgins assassination. He was the kind of man you would respect for bravery as well as clarity of thought and of expression. He had a tremendous command of the English language and he could use words and inflections which were extremely powerful. Whenever, in a country court, he referred to the senior counsel on the other side by saying, 'Here, strenuously to defend, is Mr Ernest Wood from Dublin,' Wood or any counsel that came from Dublin would be finished in the eyes of the jury! I was to use that same ploy to good effect in several cases afterwards.

We never learned anything practical in either UCD or King's Inns. I was fortunate because I had Paddy McGilligan, Michael Ryan and Dan Binchy as mentors.

I was lucky in the King's Inns to be taught by the late Frances Moran, Regius Professor of Law in Trinity. She was a lovely person, very strict. For some reason I had made up my mind that I wouldn't answer any questions in class (we were asked questions at every third lecture about the previous two). She got fed up with me saying 'I don't know' and would pass over me altogether. One day she came in and said, 'I have often thought that Justinian would not have been half the man he was were it not for his beautiful wife, Theodora. Does anybody know anything about Theodora?' I shot up the hand and told the story of Theodora, which I'm sure shocked a good many people, and she looked at me and said, 'Accurately, if indelicately, told.' From that day, we became friends.

I went for election for the first time in 1937 and, to my surprise, saved my deposit down in my old north Mayo constituency. Ultimately, at the sixth time of standing, I was elected in 1954. When I reached the Dáil, two things occurred to me. One was that, when I was first defeated in 1937, I had thought it was a national catastrophe that a man of my talents had been kept out of parliament, but here it was still functioning, albeit badly. The other was that I was horrified at the lack of attention that was being paid to legislation; it was all letter-writing and clinics. I have never actually held a clinic. Clinics, you see, are a fraudulent operation – fraudulent in the best sense of the word, in that everybody, of whatever political persuasion, comes to them. I was more of a community person. I was interested in local drainage, land reclamation, rural electrification and the provision of these everywhere. It was I that started the Tidy Towns competition. I remember making an almost violent speech against that monstrosity called An Tóstal. I said that bunting or bowls of light would not bring tourists to this country if we did not tidy up our towns and get rid of derelict sites.

I never wrote a speech. I would be travelling from one chapel to another on the political scene and I would make a different speech at each chapel, because I would make it up as I went along in the car, talking aloud to myself. I did the same thing with law later. I always had a tendency for speechifying and declaiming. Our professor at St Muredach's, the late Father John Murphy, was a brilliant man who inculcated a love of language in us by the way he read poetry to us and the way he got us to read to him. He never corrected an essay – you had to stand up and read it out to him. In February of my Leaving Cert. year, he had given us a free-style essay. We could choose any literary or historical character and write about him or her. I chose, for better or worse –

worse, as it happened – Catherine the Great of Russia. What my attraction to her was, I don't know, because she wasn't very attractive, but I stood up and said my little piece. He told me to read the last sentence again. I repeated it, but it was obvious that I had changed it, so he said, 'Show me that. It's not the same as the first time.' I handed him the copybook and there it was – 'Patrick J. Lindsay, 4 September 1927'. I had never written an essay; I had spoken them all. Father Murphy went mad, but he apologised years later when I was addressing a meeting in his parish in Lacken, north of Killala. He said he had been quite wrong not to have given me full credit for having performed so well for nearly five years.

I eventually became parliamentary secretary for education and the Gaeltacht. John Costello's idea at the time was that, after a respectable lapse of a few months, he would slip me into education as a full-time minister and let General [Richard] Mulcahy go into the Gaeltacht, but it didn't work out that way. I was in the secondary education branch in Hume Street with the late Seamus Breathnach and a girl called Betty Hunt. We were in this rather dark room and nobody came near us for three months. Nobody. I said to Seamus Breathnach, 'Maybe they think we're photographers developing pictures in this room.' We did nothing, absolutely nothing.

Eventually, I became Minister for the Gaeltacht and I went up to Earlsfort Terrace. I didn't get on too well with the secretary, who had been appointed by Mulcahy. I should have been given my own appointment, but he had forgotten to appoint an assistant secretary, so I appointed a fellow called Sean Glynn from Cong who had been a land commission inspector.

A very interesting thing happened in 1969. I decided to leave North Mayo and stand for election in Dublin. I thought the worst thing that could happen to me would have been to be elected to a Dublin constituency, because I was not a Dublin man. I was a country guy. I loved to look at the houses on the side of the hills and recognise whose they were. There is great philosophy in the country home and the country pub. I had a famous set-to in the Dáil with Donogh O'Malley about country life when I was defending the small schools. I was singing the joys of watching the frogs jumping out of the ditches, which is a well-known phenomenon – frogs leaping out onto the road after heavy rain. There were a lot of country deputies who thought I had a lot of drink taken when I made that speech.

I was arguing for the retention of the country school, because there was a different kind of education to be got, going to and coming from the school. You could enjoy the seasons, whereas now children are all locked up in a bus or a Hiace van. They see nothing. Even stealing carrots or onions out of someone's garden is an education in its own way. It was the law of survival and, of course, what grew in somebody else's garden was always sweeter than your own …

I have enjoyed everything I have done in my life, even the forbidden things. I have met lovely people and I firmly believe that the greatest thing anyone can achieve in life is the making of good and sincere friends – and keeping them.

PATRICK LYNCH

Patrick Lynch (1917–2001) was born in Dublin
and educated in the Catholic University School,
Dublin; University College Dublin; and Cambridge
University. He worked in the Irish civil service
before taking up academic life in University
College Dublin in 1953 where he rose to the
position of Professor of Political Economy. He
was made director of a major survey of Ireland's
educational needs, which culminated in the
influential 1965 report, *Investment in Education*.
He later became chairman of Aer Lingus and
wrote extensively on economic planning. He
was generally recognised as one of Ireland's most
distinguished economic thinkers in the latter half
of the twentieth century. Like his good friend
Ken Whitaker, he was an extremely gracious
and humble man. Every time I featured him on
a radio programme, I would be sure to receive

a handwritten note of gratitude within days. His contribution here is the basis of his paper to the 1993 'Tinakilly Senate' (see 'Hilda Tweedy') when he put a challenging question to his audience.

Is Economic Growth Enough?

Ireland has seen vast changes over the past seventy years. Some of these have been for the good, some not. Our historians often judge our performance too harshly, though, indeed, there have been aspects of that performance of which we have little reason to be proud.

Let me begin with our greatest achievement, something we often overlook. We have preserved democratic government in circumstances that have no parallel, that I am aware of, anywhere else in the world. The victors in a bitter civil war governed with consent from 1922 to 1932. The vanquished in that conflict after some years became a peaceful parliamentary party, formed a government in 1932 and survived for sixteen years until 1948. During those years, representatives of their opponents in the Civil War formed the main opposition party. From the beginning of the State, the foundations of an efficient and honest administration were laid.

Within the context I have just described, substantial and material progress was made, as most Irish economists would agree. But have we let the economists away with too much? We must, of course, encourage and promote economic growth, but have we been concerned more with the quantity of that growth than with its quality?

The development of any society is, I believe, far too important to be left exclusively to the economists. An increase in economic growth is not the only measure of achievement. As the American economist Herman Daly observed: 'If people die of exposure to pollution, their funerals and burials add to gross national product.' Economics has been drifting away from the other social sciences for the past forty years. Price theory cannot apply to the environment. It is absurd for some economists to claim that everything must have a price. You will recall Oscar Wilde's cynic who knew the price of everything and the value of nothing. Keynes regarded economics as a moral science, as did Marshall and Pigou, whose book *The Economics of Welfare* examined the disutilities of the market economy, explaining why firms which profited from their smokey chimneys should compensate those whose clotheslines were victims of the soot.

In the measurement of growth, compromises are essential. Uncertainty is part of the human condition.

We must begin by agreeing on the kind of environment we want and measuring the costs of maintaining it. Within that context, let market forces prevail. Economic theory has precise methods for forecasting change when people are motivated by competition for direct monetary or material reward and when outside factors do not intrude on the market. In the real world, however, such conditions cannot exist over any considerable period of time. The great economists, who were also wide-ranging thinkers, such as Adam Smith, Marx, Pigou, Marshall, Keynes and Joan Robinson, all made social and political assumptions. Change is continuous. The real world is more complicated than the simple, static equilibrium assumed by many economists. Brendan O'Regan accepted the inevitability of continuous change by adapting to a new situation in 1960 when the long-range jet aircraft began to overfly Shannon. He created a new industrial region at Shannon while others were whining about a past which had already become part of history. Today we need men and women such as Brendan O'Regan in a new situation to help the renewal of the spirit of Ireland.

The classical economists from Adam Smith onwards extended their analysis outside the narrow realm of economic facts because national policy-making must draw from a variety of disciplines – from the sociologist, the economic historian, the administrator and others. In the early years of this State, many aspects of public policy were unduly influenced by able civil servants and economists whose background and training had closed their minds to most ideas outside the British liberal and laissez-faire tradition. We were rescued from economic and social stagnation by the Whitaker programme that was published in 1958. In many ways, that survey was a reminder that economic growth, however essential, is by itself not enough. Today the fashionable word is privatisation. Many economists are enthusing about the wild race towards an unfettered, unrestrained, free-market economy which worships an unthinking consumerism, inspired not by considerations of social responsibility but by a desire to grab the fast buck and let tomorrow look after itself.

In general, we have been slow to adapt to this concept of continuous change. Arthur Griffith's belief that political independence implied economic independence lived on until it no longer made sense and was dispelled by the Anglo-Irish free trade agreement and membership of the European Economic Community. Progressive industrialisation and television are changing

Irish institutions so rapidly that they may be unable to meet the pace of that change, just as in the nineteenth century England was unprepared for the vast social changes produced by the technological revolution that made possible the Industrial Revolution.

Bertrand Russell wrote that 'technological change, like an army of tanks that has lost its driver, advanced blindly, ruthlessly, without goal or purpose'. This is because the humanities have not generally created a culture adjusted to an industrial age. Ireland must be seen in a global context, as Dennis Meadows demonstrated in his book *The Limits to Growth*. We are using non-renewable natural resources of fossil fuel, stocks of mineral deposits, coal, oil, gas and timber, merely because voracious market forces demand them.

The conventional reply to this is that a technological fix will see us through. This is a Faustian bargain. We shall sell our soul to satisfy immediate market needs and the nuclear option will save posterity when fossil fuels are exhausted. On this basis, posterity will need 24,000 breeder reactors at any one time and plutonium has an estimated radioactive life of 24,000 years. I am quoting [Mihajlo D.] Mesarovic, Pecci and [Eduard] Pestel and their arguments have not been answered. Instead of indicative planning on a global scale, many economists are prepared to accept the haphazard consumer society of the unrestrained free market.

No, we must decide what kind of economic growth we need. Its quality is as important as its size. There is no merit in producing crops that no one wants. Putting invented prices on these crops makes no real addition to our gross national product. Economic planning must be revived and adapted to changed circumstances if we are to avoid riding rudderless into a sea of make believe. This revival must be eventually on a global scale before we enjoy fully its domestic merits. There is, of course, room for a free market economy – but within an environment shaped by human reason and not designed by wild and uncontrolled forces in the name of economic growth at any price.

To counter this dangerous myth of a technological fix for solving our problems, the humanities must come to terms with contemporary industrial and post-industrial society to provide it with a set of appropriate values.

A country's broad culture must combine the most advanced technology and economic development with an awareness by its humanities of the current facts of economic life. T.S. Eliot did this for England but his vision was never fully absorbed in popular culture. Seamus Heaney is doing it for Ireland where, fortunately, the class structure is less rigid. Creative artists must keep us civilised by giving us their vision of our material and social environment. We must not forget Patrick Kavanagh who warned:

> Culture is always something that was,
> Something pedants can measure,
> Skull of bard, thigh of chief,
> Depth of dried-up river.
> Shall we be thus for ever?
> Shall we be thus for ever?
>
> (from 'Memory of Brother Michael')

JOHN McGAHERN

John McGahern (1934–2006) was born in Co. Leitrim. He became a primary-school teacher in Drogheda and Dublin before he was dismissed on the instruction of the Archbishop of Dublin following the publication of his second novel, *The Dark*. He subsequently taught in London before returning to Ireland to pursue a highly successful career as a writer of novels and short stories, including *Amongst Women* and *That They May Face the Rising Sun*. He also wrote an autobiography, *Memoir*. His contribution here comes from his 1993 *My Education* interview.

Life in the Barracks

My mother was a very gentle sort of person. She came from a very clever family, but they were poor and they came from the mountains. She was the first person from that mountain ever to take up the King's Scholarship, but I think that it was a hard thing for her, in that she was uprooted from her own class and sent to boarding school in Carrick-on-Shannon. She had seven children in nine years, and then she died. We had a farm as well because in those days it was easier to buy a farm in the countryside than it was to buy a house – you had to buy the land with the house – so she had a very busy life.

My father was a garda sergeant and again it was a very strange house in the sense that we used to go to the barracks in the school holidays and he would come to the farm on his days off. He was stationed about 22 miles from home and of course there were no cars then. He often used to come on wet nights and I remember still the blue glow of the carbide lamp on his bicycle and its strange hissing noise.

I had a distant relationship with my father. He was an only child himself and didn't relate very easily with people. To a certain extent I suppose he was, with the great influence of the Church at the time, very much a kind of symbol of God the Father. My father was very conventional in the sense that he would do whatever would be approved of. He was exercising the law and he was going to see that he set an example, first and foremost.

There was a lot of superstitious talk then. For instance we were told that the sun danced in the heavens for the joy of the resurrection at Easter. I was always getting up early to see if the sun actually danced. I heard so much about heaven that I went in search of it. We had an old rushy hill at the back of the house and I remember climbing it and being terribly tired and thinking I would never get to the top. Eventually I reached the top and there was a valley and an enormous disappointment to find another hill at end of the valley. I remember falling asleep and alarming everybody because they couldn't find me.

My mother died when I was ten. When news of her death came, I was shattered. Our farm was sold and we went to live with my father in the barracks. There was a succession of maids, as they were called then, or servant girls that looked after us.

The barracks was a very interesting place. We lived in the living quarters and all the activities of the police station actually happened in the house. It became part of our domestic lives. We would see the few prisoners that were there and we would witness the routine of the barracks. Nobody had anything much to do. They used to cycle around the roads and they used to write reports, which I think were one of my first glimpses of fiction. They used to call them the patrols of the imagination! On wet days they would hole up in some house, but then they would have to pretend that they had cycled and had to dream up what they had seen along the way. These reports were quite long, often a page and a half of the foolscap ledger. Often in the evenings the policemen would be bored, because one of them always had to be in the barracks. They would come up to play cards in the living room. We would hear them thumping up the stairs with their bed in the morning and taking it down again at night, where they slept beside a phone that never rang.

There would be enormous excitement on a court day when they would all be polishing themselves up. They had to go into town to the court and they would put a few bets on the horses. There would also be great excitement when the superintendent came on inspection. He used to line them up and comment on their dress and that sort of thing.

They also had to measure the rainfall. There was a copper rain gauge out among the cabbages in the garden and that was one of the daily rituals. There were a whole lot of pointless ceremonies. They had to put out the thistle, ragwort and dock posters and notices about dog licences, too.

FRANK MITCHELL

Frank Mitchell (1912–1997) was born in Dublin. He attended Trinity College Dublin where he was diverted from his initial pursuit of an arts degree into the natural sciences, mainly through the influence of a number of mentors who crossed his path. His distinction in a number of fields – zoology, geology, archaeology – led to his appointment as Professor of Quaternary Studies in Trinity in 1963. He was president of the Royal Irish Academy from 1976 to 1979. He wrote extensively on the Irish landscape, publishing books such as *The Way That I Followed: A Naturalist's Journey around Ireland*, *Reading the Irish Landscape* and *Where Has Ireland Come From?* As a scholar of international renown, he worked until his mid-eighties – 'I have this incredible curiosity – I can't leave a thing alone.' When I invited him to be part of the 1993 'Tinakilly Senate' (see 'Hilda Tweedy'),

he delivered a hard-hitting and challenging paper.
This is an excerpt from that paper.

Throw away the Begging Bowl and Learn to Co-operate

In the west of Ireland in the early decades of the nineteenth century, some Protestant efforts were made to proselytise the undernourished local populations by offering food and succour, provided the Catholic faith was renounced. The bowl held out was not for begging, but rather was full of nourishing soup. The offer was widely spurned, even though the local standard of food was about that of Somalia today.

What has happened to us that we are now holding out not a bowl but a begging basin to the European community? In the early nineteenth century we were crushed by poverty; today we have ideas above our station. We have been overwhelmed by the demands of the consumer society that sprang up in the sixties, and are pressing that our standard of living, already far above that of the Third World, and far above that which the resources of the earth will be able to maintain, shall be raised still higher.

I know that Irish society today is separating out, with the cream of the two-income families rising to the top of the thin milk of unemployment at the bottom.

I know that the unemployed are deprived in many ways, but it is a relative deprivation compared with the lot of the unemployed in the Third World, or with the unemployed in Ireland sixty years ago. My mother was no great admirer of Éamon de Valera, but she used to say that at least he put shoes on the bare-footed begging children in Grafton Street. The begging children are still in Grafton Street, but their current standard of living is far above that of the Third World. In that world it is estimated that 1 billion people live in absolute poverty, and 600 million on the margin of starvation. Not long ago I heard the head of an Irish semi-state company tell a conference that we could not rest easily until we had raised our standard of living at least to the level of that in Germany today. This was dangerous nonsense because that standard of living is only achieved by recklessly raping the energy of the earth.

We cannot say how long those resources will last, for it is dependent on population numbers – how many people will be demanding a share of those resources. The United Nations World Population Forecast says that the present earth population of 5.5 billion will almost double to 10 billion in 2050. Surveys between 1984 and 1992 in the Third World repeatedly reveal large amounts of unwanted child-bearing. Worldwide family planning programmes could reduce the rate of population growth, but this is an issue that no one will face up to. At the much-heralded recent UN Conference in Brazil on environment and development, the heads of most governmental delegates were firmly gagged in the sand.

It is alleged that if our begging bowl is filled then numerous jobs will be created and unemployment will fall. But if you press those responsible for running our economy as to where the jobs will arise, woolliness instantly appears. The much talked about 'Job Creation' is a vacuous expression which serves no purpose other than as a substitute for thinking. Public works are waved before us, but in effect these have much in common with relief schemes, for when the work is completed and the construction workers have been paid off, little valid new employment may have been created.

Since 1988, the Northern Ireland Office has invested £124 million in an employment programme – Making Belfast Work. The programme was intended to tackle long-term unemployment and attract private-sector investment in the disadvantaged areas of the city. But today it is recognised that most of the jobs created have been in social and community services, and that involvement with the private sector has been very limited. One critic said, 'What Belfast needs are manufacturing industries and the funding necessary to deliver such an undertaking, rather than some publicity drive designed to give the impression that a major jobs drive is under way.'

We must not fall into the same trap here. As a letter to the newspapers some months ago said,

> Employment expansion follows the identification of goods and services for which there is, or can be, a quantifiable demand which can be satisfied profitably. Alternatively, it may be possible to expand the markets for existing goods or services. But any enterprise which is set up with the principal objective of 'creating jobs' is bound to fail, and not only because its priorities are wrong.

What raw materials are abundant here at relatively low cost? Grass and its derivative, milk, are two. Today, because of the absurd policy of food subsidies, the prices of both are completely artificial. But that time will pass, and world market prices will move towards some rational level. Both grass and milk are complex chemical compounds, and conceivably both are capable of yielding other chemicals, which could serve as raw materials for new products for the chemical industry.

The soil the grass rises from is crowded with thousands of different micro-organisms, all hard at work producing chemical changes. Through biotechnology they can be made to produce enzymes and antibiotics. Scientific exploration in this field is just beginning, and it is of the greatest importance for Ireland that pioneering work in this field is being carried out in University College Cork.

This is R & D [Research and Development] at its best, and there are many similar fields in which we should be at work. Here our full begging bowl could be profitably employed. The State talks of strengthening innovative trends in our economy, but in its search for economic rectitude funding for industrial R & D has been cut by 27 per cent. And this is made when Irish spending on R & D is less than ¼ of the EC average per head of population. *Nature* has had feature articles ridiculing our position.

The new jobs, when they do appear, will have to be fashioned in a new way. The present pattern of eight hours a day, 9 to 5, Monday to Friday, and overtime beyond these points, the whole bound by rigid work practices, will have to go. Organised workers do co-operate but chiefly to defend their current working practices. This puts sand, not oil, into the production pattern. Working hours will have to become more flexible, and be spread out over seven days, not five. Such a drastic change will require generous co-operation on all sides.

Why do Irish people find it very difficult to co-operate? Horace Plunkett and Æ [George Russell] had their dreams of co-operation to aid the development of rural Ireland, but would not recognise the creamery giants of today. One can understand the acquisition of distributing firms in Europe in order to widen the field of sale for Irish produce, but the investment of capital in manufacturing firms, thus providing jobs in Europe to produce substances that could have been produced at home, is surely strange. In another field one 'Irish' company – if such a name has any meaning in the multinational commercial world of today – has more employees outside Ireland than at home. Irish banks are busy losing money in America.

GEORGE MITCHELL

Although he had been a member, and majority leader, of the United States Senate, I suspect few people in Ireland knew very much about George Mitchell (*b.* 1933) when he arrived in Belfast in 1995 to chair the multi-party peace negotiations in Northern Ireland. Three years later, he achieved what many had thought impossible: he steered the delicate and arduous negotiations to a successful conclusion with the signing of the Good Friday Agreement in 1998. Ireland, north and south, owes so much to this man. I was so honoured when he agreed to give the 1998 Open Mind Guest Lecture. His title was, unsurprisingly, 'Towards Peace in Northern Ireland' and he delivered it to a packed Aula Maxima in University College Cork. (He had been awarded the Freedom of the City of Cork earlier that day.) I was thrilled with the lecture but even more delighted when he agreed to take questions from the audience. We now had the makings of a second programme – 'An Evening with George Mitchell'. This extract was his reply to Kate, a student who asked who had influenced the senator throughout his career.

Influences

The most influential figure in my life, beyond my parents, was my predecessor in the US Senate. His name was Edmund Muskie. He served as Governor of our state (Maine), then as senator and ultimately as Secretary of State for the United States of America. He was beyond question the most intelligent person I have ever met and the person from whom I acquired the values and political beliefs I now hold. In the last few years I have come to be impressed by an eclectic variety of political leaders. I wrote a book which was published last year – *Not for America Alone: The Triumph of Democracy and the Fall of Communism* – in the course of which I spent a good deal of time with Mikhail Gorbachev, former president of the Soviet Union. While I think he made a fatal error in trying to reform communism rather than sweep it away before reform could occur, I think he will go down in history as one of the most influential figures of our time because he had the vision to recognise that theirs was a failing – and some would say failed – society and that the only hope for them was the transformation and the permitting of political and civil rights to the people of that great country. They are going through a terribly difficult time right now but I am confident they will be able to resolve their difficulties and take their place among the front ranks in the nations of the world.

I suppose that because I have spent so much time in Northern Ireland in recent years, I have been very much moved by my experience there – and there is a whole galaxy of heroes who have impressed me. I know you had Mo Mowlam here yesterday – she is plainly one of the most dynamic and inspirational public figures with whom I have ever dealt. I'll never forget the time when in the midst of a heated discussion to make a point of emphasis she whipped off her wig and slammed it down on the table! I was astonished but we soon came to know the phrase 'Well, that's Mo!' She really is a terrific person.

I think that the Nobel awards committee chose wisely and well. I believe that without John Hume there would not have been a peace process in Northern Ireland and without David Trimble there would not have been a peace agreement in Northern Ireland. Let me mention a few others who haven't got a lot of mention. The Women's Coalition, led by Monica McWilliams and Pearl Sagar, made an important contribution. And so did the parties who had affiliations with paramilitary organisations. There are many different categories. As you know, Sinn Féin denies affiliation with the IRA, but most people, both north and south, discount that denial. The Loyalist parties, on the other hand, acknowledge their affiliation with the paramilitary organisations and worked actively to maintain the loyalist ceasefire during the difficult times of the process and I believe some of their leaders deserve special mention.

I have come to believe very strongly in the power of personal redemption. Many of these men had committed serious and brutal crimes in their youth, up to and including murder, believing they were serving their country's cause, believing they were fighting for some patriotic ideal. Punished, as they should have been, they underwent a transformation in prison. Men who entered prison for acts of violence left it as missionaries for peace. They worked hard – on both sides – to maintain ceasefires in very difficult circumstances and they deserve a lot of credit for that. There is a tendency, especially in my own country, to take the attitude that, when someone makes a serious mistake, you lock them up and throw away the key. I think we have seen here that – although not in all cases – human beings have a powerful capacity for redemption and that men and women who have committed the most violent of crimes may have within them something positive to contribute to society. I feel that I have been personally enriched by knowing and working with these people and it has heightened my sense of tolerance and awareness of that capacity for redemption. For that I am very thankful and I think as a result I am a more open-minded person than I was when I came to this process.

SISTER CYRIL MOONEY

Born Josephine Ann Mooney in Bray, Co. Wicklow, Sister Cyril Mooney (1936–2023) won a scholarship to attend the local Loreto Convent secondary school, where she discovered a vocation to serve God as a missionary sister. She entered the Loreto order on completing her secondary education and left for India in 1956. She completed her tertiary education in the University of Lucknow with a science degree and she taught in a number of Loreto schools before becoming the principal of the order's school in Sealdah, Kolkata (formerly Calcutta), in 1979. Although this was an exclusive private school for girls, Sister Cyril pioneered a number of programmes that offered equal access to education to children from disadvantaged backgrounds.

She spoke to me about these programmes in an *Open Mind* interview in 1993. During her long career, Sister Cyril won many awards for her work, including the Padma Shri award, one of India's highest civilian honours. In 2013, she received a Distinguished Service Award from President Michael D. Higgins. She also won the Noma Literacy Prize, a major UNESCO award given to an individual who has contributed significantly to combatting illiteracy.

A Chance for Everyone

It wasn't too much of a culture shock to teach in India because that country adopted the British system of education when it gained independence and the British system would be very similar to the one I had experienced in Bray. However, the system hasn't evolved very much in India and still adheres to the old pattern – concentrating on memorisation work rather than developing the child's capacity to think for herself. It is a complicated system. There are thirty-three languages that are recognised by the Indian Union and a pupil is entitled to sit an examination in any one of these languages. There are also two separate systems. The Anglo-Indian system had English-medium schools. These are now very much a minority. The other is the Indian system, which comprises the Government schools, and here education is pursued through the local medium. In addition, there is a regional system run by the State School Board.

My school is a bit of an anachronism in that it is an English-medium school but we do the Indian examinations. We do the West Bengal Board exams, not the English Board exams. This gives us a greater capacity to merge into the Indian system. English is the passport to a good job in India. There are 7,000 Bengali-medium high schools in the state with only 250 English-medium high schools and, yet, when it comes to competitive exams for entry into any of the Indian institutes of technology, 95 per cent of the successful entrants will come from the English-medium schools. That's where the injustice lies. All tertiary education favours the English-medium schools. Although English is a compulsory subject in the Bengali-medium schools, only forty minutes a day is given to it and very often the teacher is not proficient in English, especially in the rural areas. So rural children have very little chance of obtaining any lucrative positions. At primary level, education is theoretically available to all but it is not so in reality, for two reasons. Firstly, the children who don't go to school are all working, earning maybe only a pittance to help the family finances. Secondly, the Government schools are severely overcrowded. In a standard-size classroom, you could have possibly one hundred and fifty children present, which doesn't do much for teacher morale. So, poor parents don't see education as being relevant to their children's lives at all.

When I became principal of Sealdah School, we had about seven hundred and thirty students. Of those, about seven hundred could afford to pay their fees. Being 'well-off' would not equate to our meaning of the word in Ireland. If they own a car, it is usually for life. They would usually live in a three-roomed flat, for which they pay a high rent. They would have a telephone. I was concerned that we were offering an education to people who could afford it – often with difficulty – but all around us there were millions of children who couldn't get a look-in at all. We in Loreto had always worked with the poor but I wanted to do more. I set out to create a school where at least 50 per cent of the children came from slum areas. They would have no English on entering school but my plan worked.

Fourteen years later, we have fourteen hundred pupils. Six hundred of those pay fees, about three hundred can pay for books or a uniform, and we feed, clothe and educate the remaining five hundred. There was some protest at the beginning when I was accused of setting up a Mother Teresa-type of mission but we overcame that by informing the parents and challenging them. The children wear a simple white dress as a uniform, which is a great leveller. We take children from age four up to the end of secondary education at age seventeen. At present, our school comprises five hundred Catholic children, seven hundred Hindu, one hundred Muslim and the remainder would be Sikhs, Animists and Buddhists.

We have also pioneered 'child-to-child' education. I got involved with some rural schools outside the city. These were often little mud shanties which local people had built in order to provide a basic education for their children. In some of these schools there were three to four hundred children attending, with maybe two masters. We met the masters of about forty of those schools to see what we could do to improve this appalling situation. Initially we sent our Sealdah children for a weekend to nineteen schools to teach the rural children, with the masters acting as monitors. The masters asked us for more time, so we sent the children out each Thursday (which is our own school holiday). Today we send out one hundred and fifty of our girls to teach some two thousand, five hundred rural children.

For any one of our girls it means going out once every four weeks but it means we have a group going out every week. Every single child from age ten upwards goes out. The ten-year-olds teach four-year-olds and it goes on so that our fifth years are teaching Class Four, which is the final year of the rural primary school. This means that in a school which normally had a teacher–pupil ratio of one hundred and twenty children to one master, the children now get individual attention once a week. That's the best we can do. I constantly remind our girls that they are receiving more than they are giving. There's none of the 'we are the grand ladies from the city helping the poor rural children' nonsense. They have to go out with a sense of humility.

There is nothing haphazard about the scheme. Our own teaching staff do a mini-training course with the ten-year-olds before they go out – how to prepare a lesson, how to handle children, how to 'teach'. The topics to be taught are put up on a big noticeboard at the beginning of the term, together with the dates on which they will be taught. Each group of ten rural children will be handled by the same four of our girls, so there is continuity. Each Friday back in our school they discuss what they have taught and they prepare together the lesson plan for the next week. They teach about the environment – water, air, plants, family, health and nutrition. The ten-year-olds are the best teachers – so dedicated and so enthusiastic. It's marvellous to see a child from a slum area walking tall into the rural school. She now has a skill and a great sense of dignity. She is no longer just a receiver. All of our children are engaged in this and they are all bilingual. They teach the Bengali children in their mother tongue and some of them who may be struggling with their own lessons are often the better teachers, because they are more patient. I have explained to the parents how this gives their children a sense of patriotism, service and compassion. As for transport, the local Leo club – a sort of 'junior Lions' – gave us a bus in which we send out one hundred and fifty girls each week – packed like sardines, three on a bench with three more sitting on their knees and the remainder standing. If that were in Ireland we would be arrested, but this is India and that is how we travel!

We have also opened up our school in Calcutta to the street children, the little waifs and strays who live on the street. These are at two levels. There are the families who have come from surrounding areas in search of work. They simply hang up a piece of tarpaulin and literally live on the street. Both parents and children seek casual labour to help the family finances. The children can come to school but on a very irregular basis. The second level comprises children who live on the street on their own without any adult influence. They are at the mercy of total exploitation of all kinds. These street children cannot sustain a regular school nor can a regular school sustain them because they cannot attend at regular times or days. We have made the school available whenever they are free to come. In such a situation you cannot have a teacher managing a group of these children. We have arranged our timetable in such a way that at every period of the day there will be one class doing a subject called Work Education – a kind of craftwork – and throughout the day we have a reservoir of fifty potential teachers drawn from our own students.

We call the street children 'rainbow children' because they unite all of us and because a rainbow comes and goes. You can't tie it down. We have about two hundred and fifty of them registered, but we might only have fifty of them one day, seventy on another. The regular children teach the rainbow children their letters by using sand in a little pot – they trace the letters with their fingers. Then we move on to paper and pencil and to books. For homework they search their environment for the letters – on buses, hoardings, etc. It is very basic but it works. Each rainbow child has their own file so, even if they are missing for days on end, they can pick up again when they return. If they are reasonably regular, they can be literate within three months. Once they can read simple books, they see the value of being able to read and they become highly motivated.

For me, this is living the ethic of my own religion – to love my neighbour as myself. We are not evangelising. I behave as I do because I want to live my Christian ethic. We plant in our children the seed of compassion – put themselves in the skin of others and feel what those others feel. We have been asked by other schools to give seminars on what we do. These other schools cannot do exactly as we do – they must find an approach that suits their environment. Each one of us has our own response to Christ's call. This approach to education is simply my response.

MÁIRE MULLARNEY

Máire (1921–2008) was a writer, educator, Green Party councillor and ardent advocate for the use of Esperanto as a world language. She educated all her eleven children at home and wrote about the experience in *Anything School Can Do You Can Do Better*. Other books include *Early Reading: A Guide for Parents* and her autobiography *What About Me? A Woman for Whom One Damn Cause Led to Another*. Her contribution here is based on her paper for the 1993 'Tinakilly Senate' (see 'Hilda Tweedy').

Effective Irrigation (A Basic Income for All)

It is a habit of mine, when I find myself in a city new to me, to investigate its botanical gardens. Some are good – Dublin's stand high – some indifferent. 'Indifferent' is hardly the word to describe one that contained a wide and beautiful lake, surrounded by flourishing astilbes and hostas while throughout the rest of the large garden the plants were stunted, wilting or even collapsed, though the whole area was served by a network of irrigation channels. A gardener agreed that the wilting plants were the supervisors' greatest problem; unfortunately, the system permitted the irrigation channels to run with water for only half an hour every fortnight.

It is true enough that I visit botanical gardens, sometimes with very happy results, but it's probably quite evident that the irrigation system is a bit of a parable. In that garden the wilting plants were the greatest problem; here everyone seems to agree that in our small country unemployment is the great evil. Almost everyone seems to agree that the remedy must be 'job creation'.

I am convinced that the remedy lies with the irrigation system, that the fundamental change we need is an unconditional individual funding to maintain a tolerable life, a National Dividend, a Basic Income, a Universal Benefit.

When this is suggested, the usual response is, where is the money to come from? I shall return to that before I finish but meanwhile I'll keep with the organic metaphor and point to the tropical rain forests. We know now, alas, that though when left to nature they are perpetually wet and warm, when the towering trees are felled the land that's left dries out and becomes barren. The trees themselves generated their own rainfall.

Proposals for a citizen's income have a long history but new technology has made them practical as never before. In limited time I can best explain my conviction by saying something about how this conviction has grown.

About 1979, I saw mention of an ESRI [Economic and Social Research Institute] report in which Brendan Dowling was asked to look for a way to get rid of the poverty trap – the trap in which an unemployed person finds that he and his family will be worse off if he, or a family member, accepts employment. Graphs show unemployment in 1979 lower than it had been for years before and lower than it has been ever since. I venture to contend that if this report had been acted upon (as almost happened), the concept of unemployment would have been forgotten by now and this country would be a model for, at least, the European Community. Dowling's calculations covered two possible systems of tax credits but found that a third, which he called a National Dividend, would be the most beneficial. It would have been possible, using the funds from personal income tax and social insurance, to give every citizen an income equal to the basic unemployment benefit. This would always be free of tax; whatever they earned above this might be taxable.

The proposal looked attractive; being myself a freelance journalist and having a large family growing up, I saw at once what a boon a reliable small income, a somewhat enlarged children's allowance, might be. But what made it much more than merely attractive was the fact that, if enacted, it would end the system which compels thousands of people to remain idle if they want to get enough money to survive. This system I see as immoral, though of course I understand it was never intended to have such an effect.

I interviewed Mr Dowling for the women's page of the *Irish Independent* and stressed the potential benefits for women working at home. I expected a lively reaction; there was none. Then, after much argument with Paul Tansey, I got a substantial piece into *The Irish Times*. This led to an invitation to go to London to a meeting of the National Council for Voluntary Organisations. After a full day's discussion, people in touch with a great variety of social problems agreed that this was the way forward and in 1984 the Basic Income Research Group was founded. Subsequent meetings had visiting speakers from other countries; the idea already had solid support in the Netherlands and Belgium.

In September 1986, the Basic Income Earth Network (BIEN) was founded to serve as a link between individuals and groups committed to, or interested in, basic income, i.e. an income unconditionally granted to all on an individual basis, without means test or work requirement, and to foster informed discussion of this topic throughout Europe.

Two things have become clear to me. One, that the key word is 'unconditional'. Dublin County Council sent me last year to an international conference trying to deal with 'Poverty and Exclusion'. Many of us know what hazards and complications beset our own SES [Social Employment Scheme] and FÁS [Foras Áiseanna Saothair] schemes; other countries are far worse. It should be understood that an individual BI [basic income] would enable all the more useful aspects of these schemes to continue, being itself a subsidy of both trainers and trained.

Just as important is the remedy for 'exclusion'; if every citizen gets this income, nobody is labelled; some may earn much more, some not so much, but there is no demarcation, no 'signing on'. Officials in many countries find this hard to imagine; interpreters usually cannot cope.

The other insight that has come to me is that, to be properly appreciated, the argument for a basic income had best begin at a very early stage. This insight came when I found my way to an especially enjoyable BIEN conference in Louvain-la-Neuve. The theme set was how to counter the common objection that a basic income would be unfair; that it would be built upon the exploitation of hard workers by able-bodied people who would choose to live on their basic income. Varied and original papers were given by philosophers, economists, and sociologists. They have been published, with additions, in a book called *Arguing for a Basic Income: Ethical Foundations for a Radical Reform*.

Even while enjoying the discussion, I began to discern that the arguments were by men, quoting other men, talking about hard-working or lazy men. Fully grown men.

When the call for papers for the next, 1990, conference in Florence included the option, 'Justifications for Basic Income Hitherto Unobserved', I offered my views on the rights of children. Though there were contributions from forty different universities, many speakers had newly come to the idea and simply wished to tell the rest what a good idea it was, so perhaps I should not be too surprised that my paper was especially appreciated by the observer from the European Commission and that it was the only one printed *in extenso* in the *BI Bulletin*.

I was so pleased with this that I insisted it be included as an appendix in a book of mine published last year (*What About Me?*) so this argument also is available in print.

Now I mean to list some of the ways in which an Ireland with a Basic Income or Citizen's Dividend would differ from that in which we are living. Babies first. We fill newspapers with Leaving Cert. results, we publish Green and White Papers, but we avert our eyes from the fact that the foundations for education as well as for love are laid in the first months and years, in the nature of things, by the child's mother, with support from father and family and friends. Whatever about equality, we know that if babies had votes they would vote to have their own mothers around. And a great many mothers who plan to go back to work find it much less congenial than they imagined. An untaxed income for all would enable mothers to stay with their children or to make all sorts of flexible arrangements with other incomed persons. When they got the offer, 60 per cent of Finnish mothers opted to exchange free creches for a small subsidy for staying at home.

I had better not say too much now about my belief that not only love and language but also literacy and numeracy are most easily learnt early and at home.

This used to be customary in literate families. Japanese mothers teach their children the first levels of reading before they go to school. Just imagine what infant and junior schools could be like if pupils were normally able to read when they arrived.

Move to second level, and to that Leaving Cert. which now dominates youth. I suspect that Basic Income would make more difference here than at any other point. If each young person knew that there was a support system, that they were not compelled to strive for points for third level, which itself might leave them stranded; if they could take time to find out what they could do in the real world, what they really wanted to learn, whether they could sandwich work and study, or simply learn by working; that if they should later decide to study, they would still have an income – what volumes of pressure would evaporate? We tend to export our graduates; I see that in Britain two out of three jobs taken by graduates did not require a degree; one in five graduates was, five years after graduation, holding a job that required O level or less.

There's another sort of pressure that makes itself felt at about the same stage of life. Male and female are inclined to pair off. I suspect that if every girl knew she had her own reliable income, fewer premature pairings, legal or otherwise, might happen. As things are, non-legalised pairings pay best; BI would put marriage on an equal footing. Within marriage, there would be fewer battered wives, if wives had money to contribute or money to take away with them to support themselves and their children.

With the frustration and aimlessness of unemployment abolished, I would hope that the depression, ill-health, suicide or violence associated with it might decline. This brings me back to that first question, Where is the money to come from?

One answer is to consider wealth rather than cash; when 300,000 people are forbidden to work, not only are they personally deprived but the whole community loses the benefits of the work they might have done. Another answer is to count the cash; one recent calculation shows that direct costs to the exchequer in payments and administration are £1.2 billion. That takes no account of the cost of ill-health, or of the loss of revenue from people who might have been earning enough to pay tax. BI is quite obviously an incentive to self-employment as well as to potential employers. It would at the same time protect against exploitation.

My own usual answer is, that it's simply a question of bookkeeping. Pretty well everyone in the country is sheltered and fed; a great many are on the government payroll already, whether as unemployed or employed in State or semi-State services. Those in other employment presumably receive more than the notional BI. Give BI to students and housewives, re-jig the balance sheet, and it will still balance.

For this intuition I am delighted to find informed support in the July 1993 issue of the *B.I. Bulletin*. Christopher Monckton worked for four years in Mrs Thatcher's Policy Unit. His team worked out the costs of a Universal Benefit scheme and found that a scheme paying every citizen at least the benefits now payable to those without other income could be revenue-neutral. Naturally, when taxpayers would get this bonus they would not get tax reliefs as well. But the British Treasury found it impossible to make this adjustment. Under their system of accounting, tax reliefs do not count as public expenditure, so their removal could not be used to balance out payments.

Monckton concluded that 'national accounts using this daft accounting system are useless as a starting point for policy formation'. I just hope our Department of Finance is more clear-sighted.

DERVLA MURPHY

Dervla Murphy (1931–2022) was born in Lismore, Co. Waterford. She fell in love with books and bicycles at a very young age and went on to publish a succession of books recalling her travels (often on a bicycle) to many exotic lands, including *Full Tilt: Ireland to India with a Bicycle*; *In Ethiopia with a Mule*; *Tibetan Foothold*; and *Eight Feet in the Andes: Travels with a Mule in Unknown Peru*. She also wrote on topical issues such as Northern Ireland (*A Place Apart*) and the nuclear debate (*Race to the Finish? The Nuclear Stakes*). Her autobiography *Wheels Within Wheels* is a candid account of her first thirty years. When not on her travels, Dervla Murphy lived in Lismore. Her contribution here is taken from the 1985 radio series *A Portrait of the Artist as a Young Girl*.

An Only Child

Every Saturday I went to confession with my classmates. I became totally scrupulous, to the extent that I kept an account of my sins in a copybook. Eventually the priest advised me to go to confession only four times a year. When I told my teacher that I would not be going to weekly confession (though I did not tell her why), she was furious. My mother noticed my unhappiness and sought the reason for it. When I told her, she burst out laughing. It was a great relief to me, but she was obviously worried beneath it all and she decided that it would be better if I stopped going to Lismore school.

My mother then taught me herself for a period. She really taught me how to learn and it seemed so much more fun. The fun ended the following January when my parents decided to send me to Ring College, an Irish-speaking boarding school. This experiment proved a disaster. I was nine years old and, having led a particularly sheltered sort of life up to then, being thrown into boarding school was more than I could cope with. I was totally miserable and wrote pathetic letters to my mother to provoke her into bringing me home. I achieved this after six weeks when I genuinely got very bad bronchitis – something to which I was prone right through my childhood.

For the next two years I stayed at home – mainly because of the difficulty in acquiring maids – and when eventually the prospect of another boarding school – the Ursuline Convent in Waterford – loomed, I welcomed it as an escape from housework. I enjoyed boarding school this time around. I enjoyed the anonymity of it all. It was great fun not being the centre of attention as an only child inevitably is, although that is not to say that my parents spoiled me. Both of them were quite severe disciplinarians in their different ways, but an only child is inevitably the focus of a great deal of emotional intensity and care about whether your vest is aired and socks are darned and all the rest of it. I enjoyed being free from all that and meeting such a variety of different characters.

Academically I only bothered with English and history. In those days, school was much more relaxed; there wasn't the pressure for exam results that we have now, so I could get away with dodging a maths or a science class – even though I was almost expelled a few times for inattention to duty as a scholar. Looking back, I think that the teachers were very sympathetic. Obviously they couldn't condone what I was doing, but I wasn't shirking work during maths or science periods. I was in one of the music rooms doing what I always wanted to do – writing a book; so the teachers had ample evidence of what was occupying my time. There were hundreds of written pages of adventure stories of no consequence – total balderdash! – but they were practice in putting words on paper.

I eventually got into print when I won the *Cork Weekly Examiner*'s essay competition for children under sixteen. My subject was 'Picking Blackberries' and I won myself the sum of seven shillings and sixpence, which was an awful lot of money in those days. I was thrilled to see my words in print and immediately went to the library to share my triumph with my father. He was very impressed, but when I went on to win the competition for five successive weeks he decided that I should retire from that particular scene!

In 1944 I met a man who stayed in our house for a fortnight but even in that short period he made a great impression on me. His name was Charlie Kerins and he was an IRA man on the run, wanted for the murder of a detective in Dublin. There was a tremendous crisis of conscience in our house. My father was of a republican tradition but he was very much 'old' IRA – certainly if he were alive today, he would not be a Provisional supporter – and yet it was very difficult for him to betray someone who came along and more or less threw himself on our mercy. It was a traumatic time for my parents and they felt that they had to impress on me that giving this man shelter did not imply that they were condoning what he had done.

I found Charlie to be a remarkable person and a good person. He seemed to have an extraordinary sense of certainty about what he was doing – not a fanaticism, but a sort of moral certainty that he was doing something good. His interests were very wide and I found him a marvellous companion. He was very keen on geography – a subject which had always bored me to death at school. I was interested in travel but not in what was then taught as geography. Charlie was also very knowledgeable on wild flowers and trees and was very much at one with the countryside, which also appealed to me. He stayed with us for a fortnight and then after some months he was caught. He was hanged on 1 December 1944. I was at boarding school at the time. His death wasn't as much of a shock as one might expect because my parents had been very understanding in the way they prepared me for it. Knowing Charlie as I did, I almost took it for granted that he would have been happy with his fate. That may sound odd now but that is how it seemed to me then.

For my tenth birthday I was given a present of a second-hand bicycle by my parents and an atlas by Pappa – which I suppose was an ominous sign, considering that I would spend so much of my life exploring the world on a bicycle. I recall on one of my cycling trips as a child resolving to cycle to India one day. Having consulted the atlas, I discovered that there was almost no water between Ireland and India, so it would be India for me. There was no more convoluted reason than that for the original decision. But having made that decision, I became very interested in India, and during my adolescence I read a lot about that country and I acquired an Indian penfriend, a Sikh girl called Mahn Kaur, with whom I corresponded for five years. Mahn Kaur's letters kindled an even greater interest in India – its people, its history and its various religions.

I loved cycling. I loved the freedom it brought and I loved exploring the beautiful countryside around Lismore. Cycling was not without its traumas, however. I set off one December morning to cycle to the top of Knockmealdown Mountains, but the journey took longer than I had imagined, and on my way down a cloud came down on the mountain and I went totally astray. I spent the night in an old animal shelter and was found by a farmer the next morning. When I was eventually brought home I was quite ill and spent the next fortnight in bed. However, the experience didn't deter me. A year or so later, I cycled all the way to Helvick Head and back – a journey of fifty miles – in one day.

During the war years it became increasingly difficult to get anybody to help out at home. I had been at boarding school for two and a half years and when I came home for the Easter holidays in 1946 my parents were on their own. I decided there and then that I would not go back to school. There was a family conference on Good Friday and three options were put to me: my parents could try to manage on their own; my mother and I could move to Dublin where I could attend day school; I could leave school and help out at home. My mother had severe rheumatoid arthritis.

The ultimate decision was left to me. I chose the last option. I suppose that basically I made that decision because I didn't want my parents to be separated, but there were also guilty feelings about my performance (or non-performance) at school. It was really a 'cop-out' for me, because if I had stayed on at school I would have failed gloriously in all my exams, in every subject, probably even in English because I had never bothered to learn English grammar. (To this day I don't know what prepositions are!) It was a traumatic time for all of us.

For all that, the next three years (from the age of fourteen to seventeen) constituted the most exciting period of my life. Once again, books contributed greatly to that excitement. I discovered Shakespeare, for instance, whereas I had rejected having him pushed down my neck at school. It was a great joy to find out how exciting it could be to read this sort of literature instead of *Biggles* and *William* and all the others. I discovered Shakespeare largely through Anew McMaster's travelling players. When he came to Lismore with *Hamlet*, that was really one of the highlights of my youth. I was so excited that I couldn't go home to bed. I had to cycle round the countryside for most of the night recovering from that performance.

Some people would say that my childhood hasn't ended yet! I know that I missed out on a lot of things that most children have – parties and group games, for example – but I really chose to avoid them as much as possible, just as I choose to avoid going to big parties now. Adolescence ended for me when I fell in love for the first time at about the age of eighteen. Also at that time I went on my first cycle tour of England and Wales. I felt that I was an adult at last and I had total support from my parents. They both encouraged me to travel as much as possible, to meet new people and see new places. My travels in England also provided me with material for my first published work since the days I had won the *Cork Weekly Examiner* essay competition. My childhood ambitions were being realised. I was on my way as a writer – and soon I would be on my way to India …

EDITH NEWMAN DEVLIN

Edith Newman Devlin (1926–2012) was born in Dublin, where her father was the gatekeeper in St Patrick's Hospital. Her mother died when Edith was five. A lonely childhood (which she described in her memoir, *Speaking Volumes: A Dublin Childhood*) led to an interest in literature that would direct her future career. She graduated from Trinity College Dublin with a first-class degree in French and English. After living for a time in Glasgow and Paris, she moved to Belfast in 1961 with her husband, Peter, who later became Professor of English in Queen's University. Edith lectured there also, in French and English. She received an MBE in 1988 for her services to literature. In 2002, I recorded a thirteen-part series with her entitled *My Books, My Friends*. Her contribution here is based on an episode from that series.

Confessions of a 'Janeite'

I am known as a 'Janeite', a passionate fan of Jane Austen. There are lots of us all over the world who love Jane's six books. I can read them once a year, over and over again, and laugh and enjoy them each time. There are very few novels that stand up to that rereading test. She is such an entertaining and witty writer. The wit is often so dense that you can see things you didn't see on a previous reading. Jane Austen has never lost her popularity. Authors come and go – for example, when I was at school, everybody read Walter Scott, but nowadays you rarely hear of him – but Jane Austen goes on giving nonstop pleasure. And, of course, her work transfers very well to film, mainly because of her brilliant dialogue.

Even though *Pride and Prejudice* was published over two hundred years ago in 1813 – anonymously – it has probably never been out of print. Its quality was immediately obvious. Readers wondered who wrote it. Little did they know that it was written by a totally obscure woman who lived in a remote area in the Home Counties. Her father was a clergyman, not blessed with a very rich living. Nothing was open to Jane, except that which was open to all women then – marriage and maternity. In that quiet backwater, she surveyed humanity and put her observations into her books in a way that has delighted and informed her readers ever since. She published her books anonymously, because at that time women were viewed as lesser than men. They would have been seen as having no experience of the world, but as Henry James pointed out, 'women have their noses very close to the texture of life'. Jane was unmarried, an 'old maid', almost, so the male view then was what could such a person have to say that would be of interest? Because Jane was unattached, she sat in drawing rooms or went to picnics or to the church and since she wasn't trying to focus attention on herself she became an amazing observer and listener.

With her brilliant wit and irony, she just listened to how people gave themselves away. Mostly we think of satirists as men – Swift, Wilde, Behan, – but here we have a woman living in a backwater who never travelled further than Lyme Regis on the south coast, or Bath to the west, who could satirise with the best of them. There are readers who think Jane's books offer a smug, complacent view of a smug, complacent society, that she absolutely sanctions vanity, snobbery and commercialism but they completely miss the irony, the art of ridicule. With irony one thing is said but the opposite is intended. Look at the famous opening sentence of *Pride and Prejudice* –

'It is a truth universally acknowledged that a man in possession of a good fortune must be in need of a wife.' Is that 'straight', i.e. indulging the view of society – or is it ironical? Jane is, of course, saying, with tongue very definitely in cheek, what a hilariously stupid view to have!

Irony belongs to the free and critical spirit, surveying what is around it. An ironist cannot help seeing the contradiction in what people say and what they do, in what they pretend and what they are. Here is the old maid living in a remote place drawing on the people she met – her own two brothers (who would both become admirals), visiting gentry, the odd aristocrat, a local illegitimate daughter, a variety of tradesmen. Her free mind played on everything they said, every nuance of their conversation, and saw into the truth. Out of that truth she made the most wonderful, witty sentences, compact and beautifully formed. All of her novels make us laugh, none more so hilariously than *Pride and Prejudice*.

Again, some readers will say Jane Austen lived at the time of the French Revolution and in the midst of a lengthy war between England and France, when there were fears of a Napoleonic invasion – and yet she makes no reference to them in her books. But she is recording all the foibles of human nature – vanity, pride, self-conceit, snobbery, hypocrisy – and because she is an inveterate moralist we get what she values – kindness, loyalty, integrity. Because these are all clothed in laughter, we hardly know we are getting them. If we did know, we would resist!

At the heart of each of Jane's novels is the heroine. In the eighteenth century, with the likes of Sterne, Goldsmith and Swift, it's the hero who is romping through the novel, but not so with Jane. In *Pride and Prejudice* we have two sisters – Elizabeth and Jane Bennett. June Austen puts into the novel someone in her own predicament – an unmarried woman who has to keep within the restraints of her society and whose only hope is marriage in order to have a home. She has no money; the family home is entailed (will not be inherited); she has a frighteningly silly mother and a witty but irresponsible father who himself married for money and escapes from his silly wife by always reading in the library. She also has three silly sisters. Elizabeth meets two extremely eligible men who have money and intelligence and has the terrible humiliation of trying to hide the awfulness of her family – 'hopeless of remedy' and 'ignorant, idle and vain'. One of the men, Darcy, is expecting little, but in spite of himself he finds he is attracted to this handsome, witty and independent girl. Jane has to suffer rebuffs from Darcy's friend Bingley, but that will all work out in the end.

The focus is on Elizabeth. Darcy, appalled by this family, is very arrogant and when asked to dance with Elizabeth he more or less refuses. She is stung to the quick and develops a hatred for him. Darcy is the pride of the novel and has to learn to be better. The near-impudence of Elizabeth's conversation bewitches him. He assumes eventually that in the extraordinary event of his proposal to marry her, he will be accepted. You can imagine Jane Austen, in that quiet house where she wrote secretly, taking up her pen to write that proposal scene! It is wonderfully hilarious and Darcy is mortified by Elizabeth's reply. She has become frightfully prejudiced against him. She is the prejudice, he is the pride. She has to learn, just as he has.

Also in the novel there is the alternative to Elizabeth – her great friend Charlotte Lucas, who brings the preposterous, fatuous clergyman, Mr Collins, to propose marriage to Elizabeth, who promptly refuses him. Charlotte sees just as clearly as Elizabeth just how stupid, vain and impossible Mr Collins is and yet when he turns his attention to Charlotte, she accepts him. Why? It is better for Charlotte to have a home and some independence and to end up with this man than to remain a hanger-on, dependent on others. And she learns how to cope with Mr Collins and be happy, 'As long as Mr Collins could be forgotten – and she [Elizabeth] could see that he was often forgotten, Charlotte could be tolerably happy … I [Charlotte] encourage him to be out of doors as much as possible.' The irony is delicious.

Pride and Prejudice is a book to be enjoyed over and over again. If you enjoy irony, you won't find anything more delicate than the irony in the books of Jane Austen.

EDNA O'BRIEN

Edna O'Brien was born in Tuamgraney, Co. Clare, in 1930. Her first novel, *The Country Girls*, proved highly controversial when published in 1960. It was part of a trilogy, succeeded by *The Lonely Girl* and *Girls in their Married Bliss*. For the next fifty years, Edna produced a succession of novels and short stories, many of which gained the author distinctions and awards. Novels such as *Wild Decembers* and *In the Forest* kept her in the front rank of bestselling authors. Even in her ninth decade she remained prolific with *The Little Red Chairs* and *Girl*. She is also a memoirist, publishing a memoir of her own life, *Country Girl*, in 2002, and two biographies, *Byron in Love: A Short, Daring Life* (2009) and *James Joyce: Author of Ulysses* (2020). Her contribution here is from a 1985 interview for the radio series *A Portrait of the Artist as a Young Girl*.

A Country Girl

Home was in Tuamgraney, Co. Clare. I was the youngest of four children (I had one brother and two sisters) although there had been a child before me that had died, so I was the fifth child, really. I was a good deal younger than the sister who was next to me so that when my brother and sisters went away to school, for much of the time I was the only child at home with my parents.

My relationship with my father wasn't very serene. It got better, of course, as he got older and as I grew older and understood him more; but he was a very restless man. He had been married very young, at twenty-three or -four, which is young – even though people do get married nowadays at that age. I didn't feel easy with him. I was afraid of him; and really, I think, chemically we were not elective creatures. I read once in [Alexander] Herzen's memoirs that the relationships we form with people – whether we love or don't love them – are always chemical; but the fact that people happen to be your parents or your brother or your sister doesn't necessarily mean that they are the people in the world to whom you're the closest. It would be humbug to pretend that. If you are close to them, then it's an extra bonus from God. I was afraid of my father, and I would be a hypocrite if I said that it had been an easy or a loving relationship.

I miss very much not having had a tender relationship with him, but you have to measure the blessings as much as the curses; I feel that to a great extent it was obviously that tension and that fear that were the sources of my becoming a writer. I don't think happy people become writers. They wouldn't bother, because writing by necessity is a very gruelling and very lonely and very anxious occupation – that's if you take it seriously. I have also to thank my father for something else which I remember very clearly: that is, a great sense of storytelling. He was a hypnotic storyteller, and I was very aware of that, but he was an egotistical man and he didn't want any interruptions in his stories. He loved it when visitors came because then he could tell again the stories that he had told before.

He was also a gambler. He loved playing cards, he liked greyhounds and he loved horses. My mother was not approving of horses, but even so there always seemed to be very restless, unwieldy horses – usually roan-coloured – in the fields. I was quite afraid of them: I remember them being broken in – and that is quite a violent thing. But my father loved these horses.

He also loved a drink and he was unlucky in that he couldn't drink very much without it having a disastrous effect on him, and on us.

I was very close to my mother. I have written about her in a story called 'A Rose in the Heart', in which the child describes her mother as being *everything* – the tabernacle with the host in it, the altar with the flowers, the bog with the bog lakes, the cupboard with the linen. My mother was someone to whom I felt umbilically and osmotically attached. I remember that when I was going to school each morning, I was terrified that she would not be there when I came home. It was very childish, I suppose, but it was a question of distance – the school was only one and a half miles away, but to a fearful child it was almost an eternity.

Life was enclosed in the way that any village is enclosed. Everybody knew our life and we knew everyone else's life. If somebody had shingles, if somebody got consumption, if somebody brought a cow to the fair and didn't sell – you always knew. I remember the great confusion and upset that ensued when we sold a cow in calf and about three days later the purchaser came back, outraged, to say that the cow was not in calf. In fact, the cow had calved without anyone knowing it and the calf was later found stillborn in some bushes. But such was our world that the whole countryside knew about the row.

Life was catastrophic. The sense of catastrophe is peculiar to a lot of Irish people. I was always nervous of something that would befall one. It was a sense of not being physically at ease in one's body and feeling that one would fall or drown or come to grief. As a result I am ashamed to say that I don't drive a car – and I wouldn't call myself a wonderful bicycle rider, either!

I had fears of animals – which is a great handicap when you live in the country. I was frightened by the people around me. I identify very much with Kafka in that respect. Dogs were a source of terror to me. They were so unpredictable; they would take fits; and I remember being badly bitten on the neck by a dog, trying desperately to escape and thinking I never would.

Also, of course, there was the fact of our own history – what one was taught and what one read at school was dinned into one as the catastrophic story of what had happened to our country.

I remember the travelling players coming to our village. When the Shannon Players came, it was a great event because they brought that much-sought and much-valued word, 'glamour', to the village. Their coming was always announced with great ceremony beforehand, but in fact the repertoire was usually the same: *East Lynne* and *Murder in the Red Barn*. There would be a comedy sketch first, then a raffle and then a play. I can still see the village hall, with black curtains over the windows and six paraffin lamps which served as footlights at the front of the stage. And on the stage those characters looked so real in their pancake make-up. I think that no theatre I ever attended in my grown-up life could assume the awe and the magic that I felt then in that little village hall.

The national school I attended was a bit 'shambolical', as Sean O'Casey might say. Our teacher was a very moody and a very nervy creature. Sometimes she would be very pleasant to you and you would be her favourite; and then, regardless of having done anything to alter the situation, you'd be a stooge – somebody to be victimised. So schooling was erratic, to say the least.

There were happy moments – especially when we read literature. Thoreau was one of my favourites, and Leigh Hunt, too. I was always in love with language – and with art, which I still believe is the one really profound religion for mankind. The only books I had access to were schoolbooks. There were very good extracts in them that I still remember – bits of Leigh Hunt, too, poems by Shelley and so on.

There were no books at all in our house. My mother was extremely suspicious of literature because she thought it was bad and could lead to sin. My father wasn't interested in books. His reading was confined to *The Irish Field* and bloodstock manuals. There was no travelling library in our locality then. There were simply no books. Once, when someone in the village actually got a copy of *Rebecca*, there was such an avidity for it that it was loaned by the page. Unfortunately, you would get page 84 and then page 103. As a result, I did not grasp the story of *Rebecca* for ages. But however restricted the diet may have been, reading was and still is my great prop against reality. As Mr Eliot says, humankind cannot bear too much reality!

When I left national school I went to a convent boarding school in Loughrea, Co. Galway. A lot of my life there was as portrayed in *The Country Girls* – certainly the actual bleakness of the convent and the regimented life found their way into that book. But the narrative is not true: I was not expelled. I was a good student and keen on learning. I suppose I did have the inevitable thoughts of a vocation – most convent girls do; you fall in love with nuns and you think how beautiful if would be to devote your life to the service of God. Looking back on it, though, it was just a whim – there was nothing serious in it. When *The Country Girls* was published, the head nun wrote me a rather crisp letter about my 'wicked book'. 'I give credence an open mind until I read it,' she said. I never heard what she made of it when she did read it – that is, if ever she did.

I think one is born a writer. I know that circumstances alter the subject of one's fiction, but the writing is there from the beginning, all the same. It is somehow that living is incomplete until it is fastened through words into a piece of fiction or drama. I always knew that I would be a writer – for as long as I can remember, I knew that I would write. I didn't know what it meant to be a writer but I knew that my reality, my life and my fate would be lived out through words: 'In the beginning was the Word …'

I wrote a novel when I was eight or nine. I wish I still had it because it could only be hilarious! I can't remember what I called it; but it was a story of a blacksmith's daughter who was very wretched and made to work very hard in the forge. One day the gypsies came and the girl fell in love with one of them and eloped with him. It was a bit like *Lord Ullin's Daughter*, except that the gypsy turned out to be a bad egg and there was a great search for him across the country. I wrote it in a copybook and hid it in a trunk. Years later, I learnt that the Brontës had written little stories as children but wisely they had kept theirs. Mine was simply lost or thrown out; I always thought I would refind it but I never did.

In my mind, I still live in the locality of my early childhood and when I write I do so with the greatest ease when I set stories there. I am not 'cataloguing' the people of the village – my writing is an imaginative reinventing of those people. If they were to write their stories, they would write differently. My characters are spectres of reality, if you like. If you look at Jack Yeats's painting of, say, West of Ireland horse dealers, you will notice how he coats them with his strange vivid blue lunatic colours; that is Jack Yeats's 'reinventing' of his characters, if you like. I would think that my 'colour' veers between red and black – because I have that sense of darkness and also a sense of vividness.

There were some marvellous things in my childhood. I was very blessed as a child and had a great inner life. I talked to the trees and I had a great love of both nature and language. I could have had a happier childhood, perhaps, but it was by no means joyless. My life has had terror and some dramatic things in it but it has also been full of rapture about many things, particularly about love and landscape.

I think that nothing ends. In fact, I have written about that very thing in a story where the child remembers 'the little stream that went "tra la la" and the clouds and that far off childhood region where no one ever dies, not even oneself'. I don't think that childhood ends. I think that the people in this world who lose touch with their childhood have lost something really intrinsic and crucial. It is hard to hold on to it in the hard, realistic world in which we live – much more materialistic than it was 20 years ago – a world in which the interest in literature is very marginal. (Most bestsellers are books that I certainly can't read. Bilge. They have nothing to do with literature! They are irrelevant.)

I hope that I have not lost my childhood sensibilities and I hope that I never will, because they are the fount and source of my writing.

SEÁN Ó FAOLÁIN

Seán Ó Faoláin (1900–1991) was born in Cork city. He became one of the most respected Irish writers of the twentieth century; a master, particularly, of the short story. He also wrote novels, travel books and a number of acclaimed biographies, among them *The Great O'Neill*; *King of the Beggars, A Life of Daniel O'Connell, a Study of the Rise of the Modern Irish Democracy (1775–1847)*; and *Constance Markievicz*. Although his autobiography *Vive Moi!* only covers the first thirty-three years of his life, it is a lyrical and moving description of his formative years, especially his childhood in Cork. His contribution here comes from *A Cork Childhood*, a radio programme I made in 2000 to mark the centenary of the writer's birth, compiled from an interview and readings by him from *Vive Moi!* recorded in 1983. If I have leaned unduly on those readings

here, it is only because they are so beautifully
written – and, trust me! – were so beautifully
read in the original radio programme.

A Cork Childhood

I was born and grew up in a house on the corner of
Half Moon Street in Cork. One side of the house faced
the River Lee while the other side led to a collection of
stables, a forge, some small factories or workshops, a
cooperage and for me the most intriguing building of
all – the rear of Cork Opera House. My father was an
RIC [Royal Irish Constabulary] man and I had two
brothers. We lived a very restricted life, the result of
which I can truthfully say is that I didn't have a single
friend all through my childhood, right up until I went
to secondary school. So the Cork Opera House was an
escape out into the world. Mark you, it was a dramatised
and sentimentalised world, because the plays that came
there were not the very best of plays. They were put
on by touring groups from London who brought very
popular plays which people enjoyed. My world centred
on the Opera House. I can remember walking down
that street one afternoon and seeing a beautiful silver
and gold coach drawn by four white ponies. It was
straight out of Cinderella. The coach and ponies would

have to be tackled outside before going onstage. It wasn't at all extraordinary to me. I mixed up reality and the play. Had I continued in that world of imagination it would no doubt have made me unfit for any kind of real existence.

My parents were very ambitious for their children and wanted to make a few pounds so that they could provide us with an education, so they took in lodgers from the Opera House. My mother always called them *artistes*. I remember my father saying one day when he had been chatting with this handsome man – 'A very nice man. He is the ghost of Hamlet's father.' So I might be talking to Long John Silver or have Simon Legree from *Uncle Tom's Cabin* help me with my arithmetic homework. Indeed, Long John Silver's Latin translations got me into trouble at school because they were so awful. It was another world.

[He reads from *Vive Moi!*]

Has anyone heard of the great Kentucky play *Mrs Wiggs of the Cabbage Patch*? She used to come down to our kitchen every morning, plump in a pink kimono, for a cup of hot tea with my mother and a dekko at the *Cork Examiner*. It was to her my father announced one morning, with sad solemnity, that during the night His Majesty King Edward VII had died. Mrs Wiggs sank to the floor in a beautiful faint. I recall with tenderness a lovely young creature, whose name I never knew, the only woman whose empty Players' Navy Cut cigarette carton I have kissed with tears, and the only woman I have ever personally known to be sawn in two every night, by an illusionist known as The Great Lafayette.

Although my father was an RIC man, we lived in poverty. Nothing illustrates this more than The Coat (I always refer to it in capital letters). It was part of my mother's efforts to economise. Instead of sending us to a tailor, she got an old tunic of my father's. It was made of some kind of felted wool – it would almost keep out a bullet! The material was so strong and rigid that when she had The Coat finished, the sleeves were like tubes. It was the most comical object imaginable. I wept, of course, but she insisted I had to wear it to school where even the most ragged boys from the lanes of Cork laughed their heads off at the sight of me. She had to give in eventually and she offered it for sale to the Bottle Woman who came around to buy empty bottles. The Bottle Woman wouldn't even give my mother sixpence for The Coat, not five pence, nor three pence. My mother wouldn't sell it for a penny so she said, royally, 'I'll give it to you for a handsel.' The poor Bottle Woman had to take it and probably threw it in a heap somewhere. It was a symbol of our penury.

Our first school was a crumbling old building comprising two huge rooms. It was the Lancastrian school, so-called after the two British educationists, Lancaster and Bell, who instituted it. We called it 'The Lancs' and it was as cracked as blazes.

[He reads from *Vive Moi!*]

My school has often since reminded me of Lowood School in *Jane Eyre*, because in spite of the cold, the dirt, the smells, the poverty and the vermin, we managed to create inside this crumbling old building a lovely, happy, faery world. And when I say 'we' I mean the brothers and ourselves, because those brothers were brothers to us, and I think we sincerely loved them. After all, they were not much more than boys themselves, country lads with buttermilk complexions, hats so much too big for their heads that if Providence had not supplied them with ears to keep them up, they would have extinguished their faces; hands as big as and still rough from the spade, feet still heavy from walking the clay. They were entirely unselfconscious, which did not prevent them from blushing like girls in the presence of adults. They had nothing at all of the keep-the-boy-in-his-place attitude that I became familiar with later on in my secondary school.

In general it is their simplicity that I recall now: their jokes that were not made simple for our benefit but were born simple of simple parents; the hearty way they used to kick ball with us in the yard, just like kids themselves – the ball, of course, being a bit of stick or, again, a lump of paper tied around with twine; their innocent inquisitiveness about our home lives, we being city boys and they being country boys; and their natural piety that threw a benignity over all our days. I recall their general and particular innocence with a general and particular delight. I once wrote a childish essay on 'Fishing' for my Brother Magnus, in which I described cheekily how I went fishing up the Lee and fished up a girl. I can still see three or four of them crowding over this essay, full of joy, gloating in their superior knowledge of worldly wickedness. As I was only about eleven or twelve I naturally did not understand why they kept looking at me as if I were one of the Borgias. To reverse the roles, how wicked Brother Patrick made us feel when he began to warn us about the temptations of summertime, and how he actually had heard that some little boys went swimming without any bathing togs at all. But in general it was innocence versus innocence, as when Brother Josephus asked each one of us to bring a book to start a library and I brought Kingsley's *Water Babies*, with a picture of baby mermaids on the cover. When he refused to accept it, and indeed was rather cross about it, three or four of us gathered about the book, scratching our heads to know what on earth was wrong with it. 'Sure, what is it anyway but an ould book about babies?'

I know I am doing them all an injustice, and doing those years an injustice too. They were happier, and these teachers (generally) more kind than I can ever suggest. The lovely thing about that time was that the days had no aim, no object: we did not go to school in order to get somewhere; we just went to school. Later, when we went up to the secondary school, all this changed. Ambition reared its nasty nose there. Up there we were pressed every day to eat the apple of knowledge which gives one power over good and evil, and makes the world fall into fractions, and makes everything not an end but a means to some end, always invisible, padding out of sight around the corner. End? We knew nothing about ends in the Lancs. We just learned because we liked to learn, as we came to school because we liked to come to school. What end is there anyway to child education except to learn a few necessary technical things and after that to shock the intelligence, stir the sensibilities and warm the imagination into some sense of the mystery, horror, and beauty of life?

There was an annual escape from the penury of Cork – summer days spent on my Aunty Nan's farm near Rathkeale in Co. Limerick. And what did I do in Rathkeale?

[He reads from *Vive Moi!*]

I did nothing. I sat by a well and saw a spider race
with delicate legs across the cold water from out
of his cold cavern. I did the rounds of a Pattern
(that is, a place dedicated to a Patron Saint) at the
Holy Well of Nantenan near Ballingrane, with
scores of old women come from long distances
in their pink carts to pray as they circled, and to
hang when they finished a medal or a bit of cloth
on the sacred thorn tree by the well until it looked
as ragged as a servant's head in curling-papers in
the morning. I saw a line of cows pass along a
road, their udders dripping into the dust. I went
with Uncle Tom, each of us seated on a shaft of
the donkey cart, jolting out to his bits of fields in
the Commons near Lough Doohyle, taking with
us for the day a bottle of cold tea and great slices
of wheel cake cooked in a bastable, plastered
with country butter and cheap jam. While, all
day, he went slowly up and down ridges on one
knee thinning turnips, I wandered. I saw a row of
twenty poplars whispering to the wind. I picked
and chewed the seeds of the pink mallow. I saw
how the branch of a thorn tree in the armpit of an

alder had worn itself and its lover smooth from squeakingly rubbing against it for forty years. I saw an old ruined castle and a Big House with the iron gates hanging crookedly from its carved pillars. And all the time away across the saucer of the lake there was the distant church spire of Rathkeale, like a finger of silence rising from an absolutely level horizon.

You see? Nothing! A fairy tale, a child's memory, a cradle song, crumbs in a pocket, dust, a seed. I lay on my back among lone fields and wondered whether the cloudy sky was moving or stopped. Childhood, boyhood, nostalgia, tears. Things no traveller would notice or want to notice but things from which a boy of this region would never get free, things wrapping cataracts of love about his eyes, knotting tendrils of love about his heart.

BRENDAN O'REGAN

Brendan O'Regan (1917–2008) was born in Sixmilebridge, Co. Clare, and followed his father into the business of hotel management, eventually taking charge of Foynes and Shannon airports. He declared Shannon would be 'the airport of the future' and, with remarkable zeal, built up its catering business, pioneered the duty-free shops, and created the tax-free industrial zone and the Shannon College of Hotel Management. In later years he turned to peace strategies, founding Co-operation North and becoming chairman of the Irish Peace Institute. He also became active in the renewal of community in his native county. His contribution here is an excerpt from his 1994 interview for the *My Education* radio series.

Developing Shannon

At the request of Mr Lemass, I was offered the job to set up the restaurant in Foynes in 1942. So I found myself, at twenty-five years of age, being offered a contract to take over the small restaurant from the BOAC, or British Imperial Airways, as they were known. I am told that [Éamon] de Valera had gone there in the early days when it was still run by British Imperial Airways and he wrote on a file, 'We should run this.' The restaurant was a vital ingredient in presenting a new image of ourselves to the people from America and Europe who were using the restaurant at that time. British Imperial Airways had three hundred staff there and when I first went there I felt it was almost like a British colony. One of the things that drove people like me and Joe Lucey and some of the other people who worked with me there at the beginning was the attitude of 'We'll show them what the Irish can do', because people had a very serious inferiority complex in Ireland at that time vis-á-vis the British.

We had no management institutes and we were operating on an import substitution experiment, which wasn't working very well because you cannot industrialise in a small space. The department, under John Leydon in those days, had purchased the Mount

Eagle Arms and it had to be remodelled in the winter of 1942. Fortunately for me, I got to know John and Putzel Hunt, very cultured people who eventually donated their great collection to the nation. When I saw their house I said, 'This is what I want the restaurant to look like.' The British had appointed Lord Headford as their station manager. 'That was an astonishing meal,' he said to me one day. 'You Irish are very good at doing things once or twice, but you never keep things going.' That was of tremendous advantage to me, because I repeated it every year at our annual general meeting. Young people should know that the biggest driving force for the Irish in those days was their love of Ireland.

John Leydon was special – he had a great sense of idealism and of sheer patriotism. I met a lot of civil servants over the years and they do an awful lot behind the scenes. They must share a lot in our success in the sales and catering service, because they gave me the freedom to do what I had to do. I would not have had that freedom without the backing of Lemass and Leydon who regularly came to Foynes. John Leydon would ring up on Christmas Day to find out how things were. He was quite extraordinary. He was secretary to the Department of Industry and Commerce and, during the [Second World] War, he and others in the department would have been the brains behind helping Ireland survive, despite the fact that we couldn't get many supplies; however, his colleagues were men of great vision. They saw clearly that the manner in which we had been cut off from the rest of the world would be eliminated by the age of air travel.

I had only been in Foynes a little over a year when the battle between the sea plane and the land plane was won by the land plane. At that stage the Irish government were backing both Foynes and Rineanna [later Shannon Airport] and had begun to build the terminal building at Foynes. I ran that for about three or four years until it became a children's hospital. We called it the Foynes Country Club and it was filled with people coming on sea planes from England and booked for five meals a day, all through Lunn's travel agency. One can imagine how important that was to people who had been living on rations!

For a period I found myself running both the restaurant at Foynes and the new restaurant at Rineanna. The new Rineanna was really an extension of the Old Ground Hotel, because we didn't have equipment there and it was run with supplies sent from the Old Ground, with Maggie McArdle, the cook from the Old Ground, being the behind-the-scenes chef.

The duty-free shop idea, which has spread around the world, began out of necessity. One winter, it began to look as if the catering service was going to lose money and there was a fierce necessity to find a new way of bringing in more money. The idea had been initiated by the government at an international conference in San Francisco where, in order to draw attention to Ireland's willingness to act as a major link on the way to Europe, they declared Shannon a free airport – not quite knowing what a free airport would be. The fact that they had done that made it possible for me to come up with the idea of selling duty-free liquor and cigarettes. The Bunratty Castle and the Rent-a-Cottage ideas came as a result of a six-week visit I paid to America in 1950 as part of a Marshall Aid-invited team. When we came back, there was some difficulty in the department about our making a report recommending what should be done, because this might have looked as if the Americans were telling us what to do. I made a separate report, recommending a whole series of things which included the Bunratty Castle complex, the hotel school and the Rent-a-Cottage scheme.

Shannon new town was also born out of necessity. We had to find a way of stopping the overfly and there were two ways of doing it. One was by promoting disembarking traffic. It was all transit traffic up to then, so the idea of the industrial free zone came out of the necessity to create payload for the aircrafts, so they would have to land for it. The town had to come to balance the industrial estate. We promoted the idea with each of the airlines and told them that they would miss out if they left us out of their schedule, which encouraged them not to overfly. I think that the possibilities that exist now are at least as great as they were in those days. The whole vision of aviation is one of expansion, as the population of the world is increasing. People are getting richer and there will be more and more tourism and more and more use of aviation, and Shannon is a vital link in this.

The Shannon story is worth studying, because we were the first generation of free Irishmen who had a chance to do something at an international level. We have a great need to do exceptional things now at an international level because of the frightening crisis of unemployment. We should be able to show what happened at Shannon as a challenge out of which the Irish imagination began to work. We now have the opportunity of working together with people from the North as they need to make a go of it on this island with us.

TONY O'REILLY

Tony O'Reilly was born in Dublin in 1936. He was educated at the Jesuit Belvedere College, University College Dublin and the University of Bradford. A brilliant rugby career, which saw him rise from schools level to playing with the British Lions in South Africa within the space of eighteen months, was mirrored by an equally meteoric rise in his business career. He was appointed chief executive of An Bord Bainne (The Irish Dairy Board) at the age of twenty-five and considers the launch of Kerrygold Butter in 1962 the greatest personal satisfaction of his business career. He became managing director of the Irish Sugar Company and Erin Foods in 1966 and, two years later, became managing director of H.J. Heinz in the UK. He went on to become chairman and chief executive of Heinz. He was also chairman and largest stockholder of

Independent Newspapers, chairman of Fitzwilton plc and Waterford Wedgewood plc, and a major shareholder in the zinc-mining firm Arcon. In 2001 he was knighted 'for services to Northern Ireland' – a recognition for his work as head of The Ireland Funds. His contribution here comes from the 1987 radio series *Heroes and Heroines*, in which a guest spoke about three people they greatly admired. (His other choices were Winston Churchill and Stephen Roche.)

Seán Lemass – My Hero

Seán Lemass is for me the great architect of the society we enjoy in Ireland today. I think there's an antecedent phenomenon about Lemass and that is that his policies were the policies of his time – he was an extremely pragmatic man – but they are also the direct reversal of the policies he initiated in 1932. I remember having a long discussion with Robert Mugabe, the Prime Minister of Zimbabwe, about Lemass – and indeed Lemass was almost a broker in my relationship with Mugabe because I was able to suggest to Mugabe that economic nationalism has a part to play in the birth of a nation but has no part to play in its continued prosperity. I suggested to him that Sinn Féin (Ourselves Alone) being the economic dogma of the thirties was basically an economic philosophy that would have been the epitaph on Ireland's economic tomb had we continued to pursue it. We needed foreign capital and expertise and we needed the boost that the Industrial Development Authority, Córas Tráchtála [now Enterprise Ireland], and other such elements of an open-door policy brought to our economy at the end of World War II. Lemass was the principal architect of all of those fledgeling industries of the 1930s that bespeak tariff barriers and quotas and economic nationalism in its most extreme form. That was a necessary shot in the arm for this country at the time and Lemass implemented those policies very vigorously and Ireland, as a result, was a highly protected economy until, say, 1950.

At that point in time there was a reversal and it was the skill and pragmatism, the decisiveness and 'let's get it done' spirit of Lemass that characterised those years when he became the full leader of the Fianna Fáil party and the most important prime minister of his time. If de Valera looked after what he perceived to be the spiritual soul of his country, it was Lemass who knew that, essentially, bread had to be put on the table and he did it in a creative, open-minded, pragmatic way. I joined An Bord Bainne in 1962 and that was one of those many semi-state organisations that were spawned by Lemass's desire to invigorate the economy. To meet with the man there was no wasted idealism, just a direct, blunt, almost gruff personality, directing your attention to what could be done with very slender resources, recognising that this country was handicapped by history and by geography (as an island) and therefore people had to generate exceptional policies with imagination and innovation if we were going to raise the standard of living of the country. Nothing was sacred. Everything was on the table. I found this greatly refreshing. In fact, I have often said that the best job I have ever had was my time with An Bord Bainne – the launch of Kerrygold, that whole period when we were trying to pull together the strengths of the Irish dairy industry and make it into the international force that it is today as the largest exporter of processed foods. I feel that the great underwriter of that realism was Seán Lemass.

There is a probably apocryphal story that is well told in Europe of his first meeting with Giscard d'Estaing which went like this:

Giscard d'Estaing [G. d'E.]
> Now that you've got into Europe, Mr Lemass, I presume you will need some

assistance for your industry. You have a rather weak structure of industry in your country –

Seán Lemass [S.L.]

Oh no – you can take it we're alright as far as industry is concerned. We don't need any help there.

G. d'E.   Well how about agriculture? I believe you have rather weak development in your processed food sector –

S.L.   Oh no – you can take it we're alright in agriculture too.

G. d'E.   *Mais oui!* Most peculiar! Our espionage must have broken down! I presume at least you will need some *décollage* for the transitional period?

(A stunned silence before Lemass thrust that jaw forward and replied.)

S.L.   Well, I don't know what that is, Mr d'Estaing, but you can take it we don't need it in Ireland.

I met Lemass quite a lot in those Bord Bainne days although my direct minister (for Agriculture) was Paddy Smith for the first two years and then for the next six years my minister was Charles Haughey who, in many ways, is very much in the mould of Seán Lemass – he has the same tone inflections and the same desire to get things done quickly and pragmatically.

There is a similarity between Lemass and another of my heroes, Winston Churchill, a sort of 'Cometh the hour, cometh the man' likeness. Harold Macmillan once said that the greatest policy-maker of all is the force of circumstances. I agree with that. I think that men of destiny are only seen in retrospect. You could argue Churchill's whole life was a preparation for his greatest hours, but really the time begot the man. It needed the extraordinary cataclysmic forces of 1939–45 to bring his genius into full public recognition. The same is true of Seán Lemass in that it was the widening of the world capital markets in the late 1950s that created an opportunity for him – with the aid of talented civil servants like Ken Whitaker – to generate that spirit of enterprise and optimism which was so characteristic of the 1960s, and which has been lost, in my view, over the last five to ten years but which happily now seems to be renascent again.

Seán Lemass recognised that the 1960s were a good time to be young and optimistic. He could be quite cynical in his own way but, as he said, 'a rising tide lifts all boats'. He was cognisant that in a small country like ours, open as it is at the end of a long corridor of events that take place in other countries and other markets, we are a very vulnerable and frail economy. But he was the beneficiary of that. His particular genius was that he could take the events of the time, take that rising tide, and shape it in a vigorous, positive way that gave us an extra percentage of growth and an extra belief in ourselves in that period from 1960 to 1970. My generation owes him a great debt for dispelling a lot of the nonsense of the past and saying that there is no such thing as a free meal. Ireland has many advantages but also many disadvantages and in order to improve our standard of living we are all going to have to work harder and more creatively. We need to abandon a lot of the cant and economic nonsense of the past and be flexible. And Seán Lemass was the high priest of flexibility.

THOMAS PAKENHAM

Writer, historian and arborist Thomas Pakenham, 8th Earl of Longford, was born in 1933 in London and educated at Belvedere College, Dublin and Magdalen College, Oxford. His history books *The Boer War*, *The Scramble for Africa* and *The Year of Liberty: The History of the Great Irish Rebellion of 1798* won him acclaim before he turned to his great passion in life – 'collecting' trees. This led to a succession of beautiful books: *Meetings with Remarkable Trees*; *Remarkable Trees of the World*; and *The Company of Trees: A Year in a Lifetime's Quest*. His contribution here comes from the radio series *This Place Speaks to Me*, recorded in 1997 at his home, Tullynally Castle, Co. Westmeath, where he introduced me to some of his favourite trees.

Talking Trees

Before we go out to meet some of the trees, I want to show you something here on the terrace. It is a section of a very big old beech tree that blew down on the estate a few years ago. By examining the number of 'rings' in the section, we can establish the tree's age, as each ring denotes a year's growth. I can tell you that this tree was planted in 1778. Twenty years later, an outbreak of the 1798 Rebellion happened on that ridge, where the rebels pitched camp, overlooking Wilson's Hospital. So this tree was a silent witness to history. I can also tell when there were years of drought, wherever the rings are narrower, or years of good growth, where the rings are broad. When this tree was about two hundred years old, its neighbours began to fall down, giving it more light and food. So for the last fifteen years of its life, the rings are wider. Hence the trees certainly speak to us, telling their own story and also acting as sentinels to history.

Here we are under the canopy of one of my favourite trees – the mighty beech. I look on it as an old friend and I call it Lir, after the king in the Irish legend whose three children were transformed into swans by their wicked stepmother Aoife and banished to nearby Lough Derravaragh for three hundred years.

I am always learning new things about this fellow. As the light changes, it creates new patterns almost every second with its foliage. As the seasons change, it is a very different tree. As you can see, it was pollarded about two hundred years ago and five new trunks grew from the pollard points. Then, in an extraordinary way, they fused together again before arching away once more. Here, in the middle of summer, everything seems bursting with vitality and the canopy is complete.

Apart from its architectural beauty, this tree is also a great feat of engineering. It is a structure holding together some thirty tonnes of wood and it is also an engine, pumping water from the ground right to the top of the tree, some eighty feet above us. This is a constantly working mechanism, raising the water in the form of sap through tiny tubes by capillary action. In order to stay alive, every single part of this tree must be covered with a new skin, or bark, which at the extremities of the canopy is microscopically thin. So, in those thirty tonnes of wood, there are miles of cabling. It is a hugely complicated engineering structure, requiring ever single branch to be renewed every year. It draws nutrients up from the soil and then by photosynthesis it turns the sap into sugars and carbohydrates, creating the bark and leaves.

These eleven great oaks are very different from the gnarled old beech. They look elegant and stately. At one hundred and ten feet high, they are the tallest oaks in the Republic of Ireland. There is a saying about the oak – three hundred years growing, three hundred years living, three hundred years dying. An oak can live for up to a thousand years, so at about two hundred and fifty years these fellows are only a quarter of their way through life. It is a salutary reminder to us little humans that they will be here long, long after we are gone!

Tennyson said about the yew tree: 'The clock that beats out the little lives of men'. They are indeed clocks and the very old ones can live ten times the span of a man – a thousand years or more. Nobody knows for certain how old the oldest yew tree in Ireland is. It could be over a thousand years. Some people would say two thousand years. The reason we don't know is because there are no documents relating to such an old tree but also because all the old yew trees are completely hollow, so we cannot tell their age by counting the rings of growth as we did with the beech tree.

We're coming down the garden path now, in the actual pleasure ground. On the left is this huge pyramid of green and from the outside it's hard to tell what it is – maybe a clump of similar trees – but actually it is one single tree about three hundred and fifty feet in circumference. It has formed layers over the years. The branches have touched the ground and formed new trees. There is a secret way in. Follow me and I think you will be amazed by what you see. This is a western red cedar which was planted about 1860. Inside, this is a magical place. One single tree had eight original trunks. When each of its branches touched the ground, they formed roots and they became new trees – a second circle of young trees around the original. About ten new trees were formed. Then the same process occurred and you have thirty new trees around the original one. So we have this secret forest in here which you would never guess from outside. It's a bit like being at the bottom of the sea but it all came from one tree, now over eighty feet high and over three hundred feet in circumference.

MARY REDMOND

Mary Redmond (1951–2015) was a highly respected solicitor who specialised in employment law and wrote extensively on that subject, as well as being the founder of the Irish Hospice Foundation. She was a guest speaker at the inaugural Céifin Conference in 1998 with a paper entitled 'Social Entrepreneurship – A New Authority?' She called for an organisation that would represent and connect those who work and volunteer in Ireland's community, voluntary and charity sectors. Her call was answered the following year with the setting up of The Wheel, 'Ireland's national association of charities, community groups and social enterprises'. The Wheel continues to flourish, with a membership of two thousand individual organisations. Mary Redmond's vision of a cohesive voluntary sector has been truly realised – in her words, 'Think of how powerful "The Wheel" will be when it is turning, its spokes accommodating the rich diversity of the voluntary sector, its centre the distillation of the great energy which drives it.' The following extract is adapted from her 1998 Céifin paper.

Reinventing The Wheel

The anthropologist Margaret Mead said, 'If you look closely you will see that almost anything that embodies our deepest commitment to the way human lives should be lived and cared for depends on some form – often many forms – of volunteerism.'

My law practice is rooted in the 'world of work' so I begin my topic from home territory. Its obituary – work's, I mean – is written every day of the week. The main culprit for the projected demise of work is 'the computer'. Arthur Schlesinger Jr, the American historian and former adviser to President John F. Kennedy, put it dramatically:

The computer turns the untrammelled market into a global juggernaut crashing across frontiers, enfeebling national powers of taxation and regulation, undercutting national management of interest rates and exchange rates, widening disparities of wealth both within and between nations, dragging down labour standards, degrading the environment, denying nations the shaping of their own economic destiny, accountable to no one, creating a world economy, without a world policy. Where is democracy now?

In the information society, the society of the new millennium, jobs are changed rapidly, as the European Commission in its Green Paper *Living and Working in the Information Society, People First* (1996), reminds us. There is a decline in continuous full-time working and a corresponding surge in atypical work and self-employment.

Yet from the beginning our civilisation has been structured more or less around the concept of work. This applied to the hunter-gatherer, to the farmer, to the medieval craftsman, to the line worker in the factory this century. Work as we know it is being systematically eliminated.

Because the importance of formal work in our lives is diminishing, because of the increasing dependencies of poverty and disadvantage in our society, an alternative vision must be found. It is social entrepreneurs, I believe, who will provide the alternative vision that is needed to complement the information society. In the community and voluntary sector ('the voluntary sector'), soul is alive and feeling. By 'soul' I mean moral or emotional or intellectual life; spirituality.

Voluntarism brings forth an energy or intensity in the community which is emotional and intellectual. It is driven by the vast energy that makes up human life all around us. To those in the voluntary sector, value in life is not solely the attaining of some aim through creating something of material value. The 'meaning of life' is not a question one can devote much time to – instead, the social entrepreneur thinks of herself as being questioned by life, daily. For the social entrepreneur, the answer consists not in talk and research and position papers but in right action and in right conduct. In a conviction that if we want to hear more of the good rather than of the bad, we must take responsibility for it. We must do it ourselves. Some unidentified 'they' will not do it for us. Nor is 'their' permission needed to take action.

What are social entrepreneurs? Not all who are involved in voluntary work are social entrepreneurs. They are harbingers of change, people in innovative voluntary organisations who devise new ways to provide support and development for those excluded from the opportunities of the information society. They identify underutilised resources – people, buildings and equipment. Their output is social: they promote health, welfare and well-being. Their core assets are forms of social capital – relationships, networks, trust and co-operation. In turn, this gives access to physical (e.g. rundown buildings) and to financial (e.g. fundraising, donations, corporate giving) capital. The social entrepreneur needs to find the right human capital. Eventually, the work begins to pay dividends. The organisation is social in the sense that it is not owned by shareholders and does not pursue profit as its main objective.

Innovativeness and vision are essential. The stakeholders are the community, the beneficiaries, staff, volunteers, and investors/partners.

Above all, the activity is not for profit. It is the activity of the gift economy. The gift of a person, him or herself, their time, their talents, their energies. When we give of ourselves, we truly give.

Ireland's 'Voluntary Sector Directory' (if it existed) would make compelling reading. While market and government sectors are often credited with advances in our society, the voluntary sector has played an essential part in creating our schools, hospitals, hospices, social service and health organisations; clubs, youth organisations, justice and peace groups;

conservation and environmental groups, animal welfare organisations, language groups, theatres, orchestras, art galleries, libraries, museums, community development and enterprise schemes; neighbourhood alert systems, and so on. There are thousands of voluntary groups all over the country. What powerful social glue!

Consider what a coming together of the voluntary experience could yield to our society:

- The incubation of new ideas and forums to air social grievances (including 'how work can screw you up').
- The integration and inclusion of persons who would otherwise be excluded.
- The provision of a helping hand to the poor and helpless.
- The preservation of good traditions and values.
- New kinds of intellectual experiences.
- Practice in the art of democratic participation.
- Friendship.
- Time and space to explore the spiritual dimension of our lives.
- Experience of the pleasures of life and nature.

The structure of the wheel of voluntarism will not be hierarchical. The voluntary sector cannot be trapped or tamed. Those of us who have met so far agree, above all, that all will break bread equally in the new identity. We see equality between groups, big and small, as vital. We see other values, too, such as autonomy, diversity and the friendship of networking.

A key word is 'change'. Coming together will mean personal transformation, together with community and environmental change. Voluntary groups themselves will benefit from greater cohesiveness, from being in the strongest position to look for and get the 'building bricks' for an infrastructure, for voluntarism, in our legal, tax and education systems, for example. 'Lobbying' will be a different experience. Education and development will benefit everyone involved.

As we straddle the new millennium, we have freedom of choice. We can influence the direction in which we go. The information society offers wondrous possibilities for creative change. Let finding the proper place and role for the voluntary sector be one of them.

HILDA TWEEDY

The year 1993 was designated 'European Year of
Older People and Solidarity Between Generations'.
To mark the occasion, I convened a 'radio senate' –
a gathering of twelve 'older' men and women who
had contributed much to Irish life and society.
They would deliberate on the theme 'Renewing
the Spirit of Ireland'. The senate met over two
days in Tinakilly House, Rathnew, Co. Wicklow, and
the resulting radio series was *The Tinakilly Senate*.
Hilda Tweedy (1911–2005), one of the 'senators',
had been a tireless worker for women's and
consumer issues for the previous half-century. She
was a founder member of the Irish Housewives
Association and author of its history, *A Link in
the Chain: The Story of the Irish Housewives
Association, 1942–1982*. She was also a founder
member of the first Council for the Status of
Women in 1973. Her paper to the 'Tinakilly Senate'

was entitled 'Ireland – An Open Society?' and there follows an excerpt from that paper. Thirty years later, how prescient was her contribution!

Ireland – An Open Society?

We live in a changing world. It is no use trying to turn back the clock to life in the Land of Saints and Scholars. We must examine the challenges of today and decide how to cope with them. We must live in the present and prepare for the future.

When our president, Mary Robinson, was elected, she pledged herself to create a more open society. She has invited to Áras an Uachtaráin marginalised groups such as the handicapped, the elderly, the gay community, the Travellers, thereby recognising their place in the community. The president has visited small towns and villages, and the islands around our coast, showing their importance to our national life, and above all she encourages individuals and small groups to use their own strengths and start their own enterprises. This is the Ireland we need, an open society, where the individual still counts, where ideas can grow from the bottom of our society and are not always imposed from the top, where there is less prejudice among the different sections of our society.

In view of the global dangers to our environment, it is necessary to review our lifestyles at local level and see what changes should be made to preserve our atmosphere and, once decided, these changes should be put in force regardless of fear or favour.

We need to develop a society where there are no hidden agendas, where there can be open debate on controversial issues such as divorce, contraception, abortion, euthanasia or homosexuality, and where relative information is easily available.

In an open society, the availability of information is essential. The suppression of information by totalitarian governments and the growth of fundamentalism in various religions is an effort to support the status quo and discourage progress and informed debate. Our leaders of Church and State are inclined to underestimate the intelligence of the Irish people and fear to put the issues in front of them. We are a pluralist society; we must learn to live together in harmony, to listen to each other and respect aspirations which differ from our own. In this part of Ireland, we are fortunate that religious belief does not lead to polarisation as in the North. It is important that the different traditions are nurtured; that, strong in our own beliefs, we respect those of others, and do not seek to impose our views on them. What better way to ensure this than to educate our children in multidenominational, non-sectarian schools? Where there is informed debate, individuals learn the courage to express their opinions, to cry 'Stop' to the violence in our midst, and to the present situation in the North.

Irish society is now made up of people from many nations, and Irish people are travelling all over the world so that racial prejudice should find no place here, yet there is some reluctance to accept 'foreigners'. We have a poor reputation regarding those seeking asylum here. Immigrants bring richness to the pattern of our lives and should be as welcome as the Irish emigrants have been in America, Australia and Britain who received us in our hour of need.

The importance of education to open up new opportunities cannot be overstressed, but is it wise to put such emphasis on passing the Leaving Certificate? Tremendous pressure is put on students, which some simply cannot take. What about the late developers? Are they to be branded failures for life because they have not attained the required points to go to university? Third-level education is important, but it is only one form of education or living. Learning is a lifelong process and we now have excellent opportunities for the adult student. More of our diminishing resources could be spent on developing initiative and self-reliance in our school-leavers, so that they can look around and create a job to supply a need, perhaps club together to start an enterprise themselves, as some have already done.

In the long term, investment of money and resources to help young people set up enterprises would be much better spent than investing in multinational concerns that set up industries here which collapse as soon as prospects improve elsewhere. Our young people are well educated and are making a tremendous contribution to work overseas. Wherever there is a call to alleviate disasters, there you will find them. Why do we not provide them with the opportunities to make their contribution in Ireland? Some time ago I remember Dr Margaret MacCurtain saying parents should examine their consciences before sending their children to university – to see whether the motive was keeping up with the Joneses, rather than what was best for the child. Are we over-educating the young when it gets to the stage that one degree is not enough to get a job? How many of the jobs available are really adding to the Irish GNP [gross national product]? Even with very high qualifications, very often only dead-end jobs are available.

PETER USTINOV

Peter Ustinov (1921–2004) was born in London. He dropped out of formal education at Winchester College and enrolled at drama school. From there he never looked back and became familiar to a worldwide audience as an actor on stage and screen, playwright, set and costume designer, film director, opera producer, author of novels and short stories and all-round brilliant raconteur and entertainer. For over thirty years he was a tireless worker for UNICEF. For this and his services to the arts he received several decorations, culminating in a knighthood in 1990. His contribution here comes from the end of his 1996 *My Education* interview where he reflected on politics, patriotism, old age and death.

Myself and Other Empires

I am life president of my own country. All my decisions are made with reference to an imaginary country of which I won't give any details but I know its history, the size of its population, its geographical situation. It is not part of any of the actual treaties – it has a veto in the United Nations because it is tremendously important to me that it should. I use it as a yardstick about what I think about very many things. I don't think this is because I have no 'roots', as the Americans call it. I don't think roots are terribly important, because I have a great affection for Ireland, which must be obvious, but I also have a great affection for Italy – I know what to expect when I arrive there and I'm rarely disappointed. Naturally, I do have prejudices. We all do and we can't avoid it. When my daughter started bringing black students home, she thought it would frighten me because she might marry one. Of course, it didn't at all, but I did tell her, 'Don't think I'm absolutely free from prejudice, because if you came home with a son of a South African apartheid member, I think I might object to that in the family.'

I don't find nationality important, because my father was German by passport and became British. One of his brothers was killed in the First World War as a German officer, another was Canadian and his younger brother is Argentinian and the sister of all those boys is Lebanese. So how on earth can I take passports seriously? It doesn't make any sense at all. I don't mind what passport I have and in fact I very often travel on a United Nations passport, to which I'm entitled. What is important is the cultural values of each country, which, as an outsider, I can appreciate as much as anybody. I can't stand patriotism, if it is of the variety which is exercised at the expense of other people. This seems to me absolutely barbarous and old-fashioned. Love of a country and its traditions is absolutely natural and a wonderful thing, but I think one can have one's roots in civilised behaviour and I find that even more satisfactory. Without wishing to lose my fascination for my own ethnically filthy roots, of which I'm very proud!

I think that parliamentary democracy is all very well, but it is in disrepute now, because, on the whole, politicians are no longer trusted as they once were, and they are in a difficult situation because they have to try to make themselves attractive. You can see that, in every election in every country, the turnout has to be stimulated, because otherwise relatively few will turn up to vote. On the other hand, non-government organisations are becoming more important, because they express real human concerns. The first non-government organisation was the Red Cross, which started from one individual's horror on the battlefield at the beginning of the last century. Gradually, the Swiss Red Cross and then the international Red Cross took shape and did something. This is now acknowledged by all nations, but no single government would have been capable of putting such a thing into orbit. It had to be a non-government organisation. We now have Greenpeace, Amnesty International, hundreds of organisations, which came into existence because they correspond to a human, as opposed to a national, need. Curiously, they are getting richer, although they started from very humble roots, just like the Swiss Red Cross. Now, if you have an international congress, the contribution of non-government organisations is far more alive and vital than that of any delegation working under instructions from a capital. I am president of the World Federalist movement, which is a completely un-subversive movement. This is an organisation which has an office in the United Nations and which is at the forefront of those who want an international criminal court, among other things.

In my travels with UNICEF, I see frightful things and I see things which are disturbing. Nowadays, everybody's attention is attracted to Burma, quite rightly, because of the extraordinary character of a single woman, who is handling herself with great cleverness, confronted by a military government of generals. Nobody's going to starve in Burma; you can eat what you want off the trees. But Cambodia's situation is really most distressing and the human race should feel a twinge of conscience. More bombs were dropped on it than on Vietnam, and now the most hideous statistic of all is that over 50 per cent of the population are under fifteen years of age, because between two and three million of the older generation were killed, out of a population which was then eight and a half million. Flying over it now is like flying over a plucked chicken, because there has been such devastation. The real tragedy of a country like that is that it is practically impossible for it to attract any foreign investment, because of the uncertainty and because of the ruin everywhere. I was sent there on a mission by UNICEF and I was very struck with the contribution UNICEF is making, but external help is not forthcoming on the scale which is needed.

I am learning something now which you really can't learn when you're young – that the human soul doesn't age. I'm sure within myself that I am exactly the same person as I was when I was one year old, or ten or fifteen. I am listened to because I look different and

I have more experience. But, as time passes, the body begins to depart from the soul – I can understand why people in the Bible wrote about giving up the ghost. The body becomes more and more strange to you, because it doesn't behave as well as it used to. I feel that, when you are born, you go to a counter which is a kind of Hertz rent-a-body counter and you say to the girl:

'Listen, haven't you got something with a slightly sportier engine?' or 'Oh! A sliding roof, I'd like that very much.'

And she says, 'No, wait, they're all out. Take that one or leave it.' And you take it and you're stuck with it all your life, and it becomes much more of a stranger at the end because you begin listening for creaks in the bodywork and there is a noise coming from the back axle which you don't like and so you drive it more slowly than you did before. And you hope that you'll keep your dignity and be able to bring it back to the counter to hand it in and won't be stuck out in the countryside with a red triangle behind you, waiting to be collected. I regard the whole thing with some amusement and am not really frightened of death, simply because I don't remember being frightened of birth. And, after all, the entry and the exit must have something in common! I'm not going to hurry the process. They gave me a new passport, which expires – charming, the word they use for a passport – on 10 April 2000. I really want to make it a point of honour to live as long as my passport, because it is such a waste, otherwise.

I have regrets, but they are not important, because you have to choose a way and if you start regretting you didn't go the other way you are wasting time. Life is much too short, which is a terrible thing, of course, but it would be even worse if it was much too long. Without death, you couldn't assess anything. It's like a map without a scale. If you start to think about what you could have done, you lose the initiative, and life is nothing but a mass of initiatives which you simply have to take. You can't get out of yourself. You're stuck with yourself for better or worse and there is no use in having enormous regrets that you are not this way or that way. You can be a Walter Mitty secretly. I am a Walter Mitty, because I'm my own country, where I have no great difficulty in suppressing the opposition. Although it's a democratic country, you understand. Of course, it is a country in which there is a modicum of freedom, but certain things are in the hands of a government, with a whole ministry devoted to consultation. I think consultation is very important, otherwise I wouldn't have called my autobiography *Dear Me* and divided myself into two. I don't give a concrete answer to any question, instead the two sides of my nature argue it out, which I think is not only more democratic but also more revealing.

T.K. WHITAKER

Ken Whitaker (1916–2017) was born in Rostrevor, Co. Down. His family moved to Drogheda, Co. Louth, in 1922, just as the Civil War was unfolding. He had a distinguished career in the civil service, rising to secretary of the Department of Finance from 1956 to 1969. He is credited with the economic development that marked the opening of the Irish economy to the outside world in the late 1950s. He was governor of the Central Bank from 1969 to 1976. A former senator in the Irish parliament, he was also president of the Royal Irish Academy. He had a lifelong commitment to the Irish language and served as chairman of Bord na Gaeilge. He was elected chancellor of the National University of Ireland in 1976. For a man with such a distinguished career – many have described him as the architect of modern Ireland – he was ever gracious and humble. I would meet him regularly on the No. 10 bus when we would discuss the issues of the day. This contribution on his civil service days is taken from the 1995 interview for the series *My Education*.

Becoming a Civil Servant

For boys who had a Christian Brothers education at the time there were very few outlets. The civil service and local authorities and a few other jobs of that kind were the only things on offer. In the very early days when I was in the civil service commission, I sat with a man who was the father of Eithne FitzGerald. Our job was somewhat like that of Laocoön, who was wrestling with all the serpents in that famous sculpture. We were wrestling with great big sheets of sticky paper on which we had to put the marks for various examinations. We then had to put them into numerical order, which meant getting all these narrow, perforated sheets and putting them back on a new background – a very sticky and unexciting job!

However, we were rescued from that because once you're in the civil service commission and want to do another competitive examination, you are hounded out to somewhere else for fear you might see the papers in advance. I was sent to the Department of Education at a very early stage and actually became private secretary to Tomás Ó Deirg, who was the minister at the time.

I wasn't too impressed with Education as a department. My impression of it was that people did not co-operate well. There were a lot of people whose main interest was not to help you but to 'walk you up the garden'. There was a great deal of unnecessary competitiveness. They didn't have enough input from outside; the kind of graduate intake that Finance and some other departments had was not available to them and that continued for quite some time.

I spent a little while in Revenue as an assistant inspector of taxes, which was another rung of the ladder. For that examination, economics or commerce was on the syllabus. I had never heard of economics until then, so I decided I had to do something about it. I started doing, first of all, a London University arts degree in mathematics and Celtic studies, Latin and law. I got some credit for the mathematics to do an economic/ science degree by correspondence, as an external student. Later on, I completed it by doing a master's of science/ economics, as they put it.

I went to Finance in 1938. I have always likened it to entering an officer corps. No matter how junior you were, you had access to the officers' mess, you could ask the general something and you wouldn't be frozen out. It was a completely new experience, an exhilarating one, to be in a place where that kind of esprit de corps existed. It was very much like an academic institution. There was a good deal of talking amongst ourselves about economic problems. There were people there in my time like Paddy Lynch and Jack Nagle, with whom one could talk over problems one had with one's own study.

In my thirty-one years in Finance, one of my great mentors was Arthur Codling, an Englishman who stayed after the Treaty to help in the new department and who became assistant secretary there. He was quite a disciplinarian; you made sure that you got your file numbers correct on your documents and so on. He was also someone who, by his own example, taught you how to mix intuition and logic to good advantage.

Professor George O'Brien of UCD [University College Dublin] was also extremely helpful to me. I was somebody outside his own immediate sphere, somebody who had never gone to university, but I was included by him amongst those he called his 'swans', the people he invited to dinner and pleasant debates in congenial company.

Anyone who grew up in my generation couldn't help but be influenced by the socialists, who got a great innings from the first Penguin and Pelican books – Harold Laski and G.D.H. Cole and so on. In 1936, [John Maynard] Keynes's great book, *The General Theory of Employment, Interest and Money*, came out and Keynes was the focus of discussion for years after that.

As for Ministers for Finance, I was there in Seán T. O'Kelly's time, and then Frank Aiken would have been there from about 1946 to 1948, before the first inter-party government came in. At that time Aiken was extremely interested in cheap money – Mr Dalton, the British Chancellor of the Exchequer, was a great proponent of cheap money. I was just a junior officer, so he kept asking the senior people all sorts of awkward questions and they turned to me. I had to endure long sessions of discussion and query and then do my own research, trying to keep at least one step ahead of him. The result was that I was able to put together – with his encouragement – a book on financing by credit creation during the last war in Britain and the United States. I cured him slightly of his preoccupation with cheap money, but we did manage to use all our expertise and persuasion against the banks of the time to induce them to provide money at a much more reasonable rate for the Exchequer on Exchequer Bills.

In the post-war period, Seán Lemass was one of my great political heroes. I admired him a lot for being a man of decisiveness. He was a pragmatic patriot, a man who was in the right place at the right time, though perhaps not timely enough. I would agree with those who think that de Valera probably stayed on too long. It was clear to everyone, and became clear to Lemass in particular, that protectionist policies, the self-sufficiency policies, were outmoded so, after the [Second World] War, Lemass began the process of dismantling it all. First of all, he introduced a bill to restrict protection, to force the infant industries to become adult. However, that was never passed, because in 1948 there was a change of government. Once he came back into power and we reassessed policies in the mid-1950s, I think everyone agreed that there was no future for either employment or improved standards in Ireland if we were relying on an impoverished home market. We had to break out; we had to sell in the export markets competitively.

We also learned a lot from civil servants like John Leydon and J.J. [James John ('Jimmy')] McElligott. We observed them when we went on trade talks or negotiations of an economic kind to London or Paris. We were the young people briefing them, doing the groundwork, but also watching how they dealt with cross-table discussion and argument. Leydon in particular was quite a fierce terrier in those situations.

In the late 1950s, we prepared the programme for economic development. It made the change from a self-sufficiency policy to an open export-oriented policy. The significant thing about it was that it was a product of the most unlikely place in the world – the hard-bitten, negative Department of Finance. People were impressed and said there must be something in it, there must really be some potential for development in the country if those people in Finance say there is. I think that helped to create confidence, that psychological factor which I would regard as one of the most important factors of production.

De Valera, who was just in his last months as prime minister, had the magnanimity to say we should publish the book and let it be known that the authorship was a group of civil servants. That was a big step for him, because other people, like Seán MacEntee opposed it. De Valera, Lemass and Dr Jim Ryan said publish and be damned, as it were. Of course, they were very astute politically in doing so, because it would have been much harder for them to embrace a complete reversal of traditional policy on their own account, much easier when it was apparently the advice of objective, nonpolitical civil servants. It was a time of great satisfaction, because most of us who were engaged in that felt that we were the first privileged generation of the new Ireland. We'd had good jobs, a good education, and here was a chance to apply what we had learned for the benefit of the country, as we saw it. That was a source of great satisfaction. Indeed, I remember thinking, going back to Wordsworth, how apt it was when he said, 'Bliss it was in that dawn to be alive/But to be young was very heaven'.

GORDON WILSON

Gordon Wilson (1927–1995), the 'ordinary wee draper' from Enniskillen, Co. Fermanagh, was thrust into the world limelight in November 1987 when he was interviewed on television following the Provisional IRA bombing that killed his daughter Marie and ten others. When asked how he felt about the people who planted the bomb, he replied, 'I bear no ill will ... I shall pray for those people [the bombers] tonight and every night. May God forgive them.' He became a member of Seanad Éireann (the Irish Senate) and was a tireless worker for peace until his death in 1995. When I invited him to give the 1993 Open Mind Guest Lecture, he replied, 'I will surely, but I'm no public speaker. Everywhere I go I just tell a wee story from Enniskillen. That's all.' Indeed it was, but that 'wee story', extracted here, and the way he told it, moved his audience to tears.

Marie

I'll tell a little story which, I think, very simply but clearly illustrates the sort of ongoing 'bouncing' that happened on a daily and nightly basis. We sold heavy underwear, lamb's wool underwear. The farmers bought it. It was made in Yorkshire and it carried a label, and on that label was a woven Union Jack, and I had decent Catholic farmers who wouldn't buy it. They saw it as waving the flag. Then the firm went out of business, and I found a firm in the County Dublin who made a similar sort of underwear, and the label on their garment said: 'Made in the Republic of Ireland'. I had decent Protestant farmers who wouldn't buy it. Now you may smile, you may even laugh, but, frankly, I didn't find that funny; I found that sad. But it is symptomatic of the sort of feelings and attitudes and approaches that people had on both sides.

I married my wife Joan in 1955. She is a local lassie from some six or seven miles out of town. Her father was a farmer. He lost a leg in the Great War, in France, and often talked about being sent home and nursed in Dublin by the nuns, and spoke very highly of them. Joan is a teacher, originally a primary school teacher, and then, for some fifteen or twenty years now, she has been teaching the violin. She is what is called a peripatetic teacher – that's the only five-syllable word I know! – in that she's not employed by any one school. She travels around. She is employed by the Music Service of the Western Education and Library Board.

We married in 1955, and got on with building up our home and family and, of course, for me life revolved around the business and, for Joan particularly, around our church, where she plays the organ and trains the choir. As a businessman, I got into the Chamber of Commerce and the Rotary Club. I played a little golf and a little tennis and played bowls twice for Ireland. And life was good. We were comfortable.

We had three children: Peter, Julianne and Marie. And then, twenty-five years ago, came the 'Troubles'. The 'bouncing' I've talked about became suspicion, and suspicion led to distrust, and distrust to fear, and fear to hatred, and hatred to confrontation, and confrontation to death. An eye for an eye, and a tooth for a tooth. But we, as I suspect every family does in Northern Ireland, always thought it would be somebody else's eye, or somebody else's tooth. And what about Marie, our Marie? Born in 1967, the youngest, the pet, maybe a little spoiled because of that. I like to think you will understand if I say she was special. People say: 'What will you longest remember about her?' The answer is always the same: her smile. She was a smiler. I don't think we have a single photograph of her where she isn't smiling.

She was not an intellectual, but she got two good A levels. Big, strong lassie; never seemed to sit down; active, into games, into music through her mum; won a Duke of Edinburgh Gold award. She loved people. She wasn't outwardly religious, but her heart was in the right place. We like to think she had a happy childhood. She was not to know it, but she was to become a child of our times. She was politically and religiously aware. Young people in Northern Ireland cannot be otherwise. I do not forget one evening at tea – she would have been, perhaps, nine – and she said to me: 'Daddy, what's wrong with the Catholics?' It's a tight question. I hope I was able to answer it fairly and justly. Something she'd heard …

At the age of eighteen, she went to train as a nurse at the Royal Victoria Hospital in Belfast. Having done two years' training of her three-year course, Marie came home on the seventh of November, the day before Remembrance Sunday, 1987 – six years ago; sometimes it seems like sixty-six. And she volunteered to come with me the following morning, as I had done for forty years, to the annual Remembrance Day war memorial service. Suddenly, it wasn't somebody else's eye, nor somebody else's tooth. We stood with perhaps a hundred and fifty, two hundred civilian people. The parade had not yet arrived; the army, the RUC [Royal Ulster Constabulary], the UDR [Ulster Defence Regiment], the British Legion, ex-service men. It was about a quarter to eleven. And we were standing where I had always stood, with my back to the wall of a disused school. We were not to know it, but immediately behind us, on the other side of the wall, was the bomb. And then the bomb …

Six of the seven people within five feet of where we stood died in that bomb. (So is it any wonder I ask myself, 'Why am *I* here in Montrose tonight, i.e. why did I survive when others did not?') The gable wall began to collapse and fall on top of us. I was thrown forward – it seemed to me, in slow motion – on top of the people who were standing in front of me. And I remember thinking as I fell: All I need is a big one and it's goodbye. I didn't get the big one.

Then the rumble of the wall falling stopped, and I found myself under four to six feet of loose rubble, and then the silence. The deathly silence. And then the shouting. And then the screaming. This was raw, naked terror. I was on my face. I was conscious that I had survived. My right arm had been thrown out in the fall and, in so doing, I had dislocated my shoulder. And then somebody took my right hand. 'Is that you, Dad?' I couldn't believe it. It was Marie. I remember thinking, Thank God, Marie is safe.

'Are you alright, Marie?' and she said 'Yes, Dad,' she said, 'let's get out of here.'

I said, 'Marie, we can't get out of here. We're caught, we're pinned in, we've got air, we can breathe. They'll come, they'll come. Give them time. Are you alright?'

'Yes.' And then she screamed. That was the first warning I had that something was wrong. Three or four times I asked her was she alright, and all the while holding her hand. And each time she said, 'Yes.' But each time she screamed. I couldn't understand why, on the one hand, she was telling me she was alright, and on the other hand, she was screaming. And when I asked her for what would have been perhaps the fifth time, 'Marie, are you alright?' she said, 'Daddy, I love you very much.' That was her moment of truth; those were her last words.

She had to have known she was hurt. She had to have known she was at Calvary's edge. And what glorious words she used as she joined her Heavenly Father. Not words of anger, nor words of hatred, nor words of selfishness; words of love. And because of them, Marie Wilson was mourned by millions the world over.

And because of them, my greatest honour is to have been Marie Wilson's dad.

BENJAMIN ZANDER

One of the wonderful things that happened during my thirteen-year spell as presenter/ producer of *The Open Mind* on RTÉ Radio was the development of a network of listeners who would contact me and say, 'There's a man giving a talk in Trinity College tonight. You should talk to him' or 'Have you read this book? It's your kind of stuff.' A particular instance in 2002 was a phone caller who told me that Ben Zander (*b.* 1939) was in town as guest conductor of the National Symphony Orchestra and I should talk to him. 'He's a really interesting man and he has written a fascinating book.' With some trepidation, I arranged an interview in the Conrad Hotel, across the street from the National Concert Hall, and spent an hour enthralled by this man's story, his views on education and his fascinating book. I hope the following extract from that *Open Mind* interview captures something of the spirit of the man and his ideas. For me, it was one of the most fascinating interviews I had the pleasure to record and over two decades later it retains its freshness and richness of content.

The Art of Possibility

I was born in England but thirty-five years ago I moved to Boston, where I conduct the Boston Philharmonic Orchestra, I run a youth orchestra, teach at the New England Conservatory of Music and I run a school for accomplished children. My father was German and my mother came from Holland. My father was an interesting man – a lawyer by training, a Middle Eastern scholar and an extraordinarily accomplished musician – and it was through him that I developed my passion for music. I left formal schooling at the age of fifteen to become the student of a great Spanish cellist Gaspar Cassadó. I was his apprentice for five years travelling around Europe and living in Florence. It was a magical time. He had an apartment in one of those eleventh-century towers on the Ponte Vecchio where I would climb the stairs to his studio for my lessons. It was a most unusual life.

He would call me late at night for a lesson. 'But maestro, I'm in bed' I would protest.

'Well, get up and get over here now,' he would reply. So I would walk across Florence with my cello for a lesson that might last three hours and then he would take me to a late-night restaurant and dine with poets and writers until four in the morning and then I would walk home again with my cello. It was very much the old master–apprentice approach.

He taught me for nothing. He told my father that if he charged him what the lessons were worth, he couldn't afford it! I was never lonely. I had some Italian friends, but mostly I was practising and working for Gaspar and it all seemed just a wonderful, wandering life! I didn't pursue a career with the cello because I had this peculiar phenomenon of not being able to produce callouses on my finger – which I would need as a cellist! So I tried several other paths and the one that really arrested me was conducting. On the way I did a degree course in English literature, going right back to Beowulf. It was enormously engaging and something I couldn't have done had I pursued a career as a cellist.

There are great parallels between literature and music. One of the things that literary people take for granted is the deep analysis of poetry. That kind of analysis has not happened with music so I was able to find some pathways into music analysis which I use in my teaching and conducting. To explain the poetic content in the music is very helpful to the musicians and gives them more vitality in their playing. Similarly, I can 'explain' the music better to a listening audience.

One of the meanings of a conductor is to be a conduit – somebody through whom the possibility of the music flows to the players who actually make the music. The conductor takes the written score and filters it through his experience, his ear, his training, his imagination, and through his body gives that to the players who then translate the score into sound. Doing it that way, enlivening the spirit and vitality of the players, is one approach. The other approach is how the conductor dominates the players with his own view and forces them to follow his will. Both are effective ways of leading. Most people follow the old top-down, hierarchical way of leadership but I found the other way of creating possibility in others is, in the end, more spirited and more satisfying for all concerned. I invite rather than force the players to find the freedom in the music – it is risk-taking and therefore more dangerous.

The players are empowered – if you hoard power as a conductor, you only get your own power back. If you give it away, you get everyone's power in return, which is very formidable when unleashed, especially with youth orchestras who play with incredible intensity and joie de vivre; a daredevil, edge-of-the-chair quality. To that end, I give every player a blank sheet to express their opinions or ask questions. I am drawing on their vast experience following a very lengthy training in their profession – what ideas they might have! If, as a conductor, you open yourself up to this 'coaching', it will be most useful. That is true of any kind of leader – a parent, a teacher, a political leader. If something they are doing is closing down or disabling those they are leading, wouldn't they want to hear that?

It's all about awakening the possibility in others and, with my wife Rosamund, who is a family therapist, I have written a book, *The Art of Possibility*. It's a clever title because we can have complete control of possibility in our lives, provided we learn the art of how to bring it into the world. For example, if, as a parent, you say, 'You should/must do that', it immediately closes down the possibility – but if you say, 'How about?' or 'What are we looking for here?', immediately the whole thing becomes open and suddenly possibility is alive. It lives very much in our language. *The Art of Possibility* is a book about clarity in distinguishing what closes and what opens possibility and if you become masterful in it you then have mastery in life. We believe there is literally no problem that cannot be solved, from which you cannot find an opening by reframing it. It is not difficult to do this but it is demanding. Finding that 'open space' is such a joy and a release.

It is simple but not easy. What we call the 'downward spiral' – the negative thinking, 'It can't be done' and all the clichés we have about human beings – causes us to get locked in a vice from which there is no escape. That breeds cynicism. A cynical person is a passionate person who doesn't want to be disappointed again. Immediately there is an opening. You speak to his/her passion, presuming it is still there. It's called 'giving an A' – the highest grade there is – and you speak to them not only as if they were capable of playing great music but that they want to be taught that way. You can speak the truth to them in that way. This book was published by Harvard Business School Press and is currently their number one bestseller, even though it's not a business book. It's about a new form of leadership, which Rosamund and I have pioneered, based on our own experiences.

The transformation that can occur is almost miraculous. When you 'give an A' to someone, it's like having an aquarium with extremely clear water. The fish look beautiful and they swim with alacrity. If the aquarium is grimy, the fish look grimy and they don't swim very happily. If there is clear water and there is air to breathe, miracles will occur. If you create a world of 'contribution' around you there is no way of measuring it, because measuring doesn't belong in contribution. Similarly, mistakes are important. They are the only way you can learn. I encourage my students to celebrate making mistakes by physically throwing their hands in the air and exclaiming, 'How fascinating!' Most of our examination systems are sadly structured in this way – trying to find out what students don't know rather than what they do. It puts students in a defensive mode. Whereas learning is such a joyful process, children can slowly get closed down.

Why can't we keep that enthusiasm – a lovely word which means 'full of God'? There's that wonderful story of the cellist Jacqueline du Pré. When she entered her first competition as a young child, she came bouncing down the corridor with her cello. The doorman said to her, 'Well, you've obviously done well' but she replied, 'Oh no, I'm just about to play well!' She knew as a child that to play music is a joy and a privilege. I gave my students a serious assignment last week – to 'come from the power of the child'.

By the way, I give my students an A on one condition. At the beginning of the school year, they must write me a letter which is dated the following May (i.e. end of year) and begins 'Dear Mr Zander, I got my A because …' They must describe at some length who they will have become, to justify this grade. I tell them to fall passionately in love with the person they are describing. It's the art of possibility. As a parent, a teacher, an employer, we do well to speak to the 'A part' of our children, students, employees, rather than to their 'C minus part'. That has to do with our language, our body language, and the things we don't say to them. Speak to their possibility; their highest side. I think if politicians did that, we would have far less conflict in the world.